WANDERINGS OF A TEN POUND POM

Anecdotes of a 1960s English emigrant to Australia

Bob Horsman

ISBN: 978-1-925590-26-5
Published by Vivid Publishing
P.O. Box 948, Fremantle
Western Australia 6959
www.vividpublishing.com.au

Cataloguing-in-Publication data is available from the National Library of Australia

1965

Oldham, ENGLAND

Oldham, the northern England town of cotton mills and pubs, where it was once reputed there was one pub for each day of the year, is also the home of my family, friends and beloved football team, Oldham Athletic whose fortunes I still follow from many miles away.

After 11 years of continuous employment, firstly as an apprentice electrician from the age of 15 and continuing on until age 26, working for the same employer based in Shaw, a small town in the outskirts of Oldham, I started to think seriously of a change in life style. It was in October 1965 that I finally took the plunge and went about seeking emigration to Australia, the much-advertised "land of opportunity". A Sunday newspaper contained application forms for a 10 pound assisted passage for emigration. Interviews were conducted at Australia House in Manchester and following these, I was granted passage to Sydney, New South Wales for early 1966. The passage was to travel to London on the night mail train from Manchester in February with a flight to Sydney from Heathrow airport the next day.

I worked from time to time with another young bloke in Shaw who was a carpenter with one of the building contractors who were sometimes on the same contracts as I was. It was at one of my local pubs one night in December just a few weeks before my departure date to Sydney when another guy who worked for the same building company told me that his work mate was also going to Australia as an emigrant and maybe I would want to pop into his local pub for a chat with him. This I did and as he would be flying out in January, we decided to meet up in Sydney after my arrival. He sent me an address where I could contact him after he arrived at Sydney and we arranged for him to meet me at the airport.

Just jumping ahead a little, it came about that he was my best man at my marriage to Lorraine in Sydney in 1977, after crossing paths many times over the years. There was however, much time to be filled in before then.

The few weeks before my departure date were very busy, with many farewells with friends and my relations around Oldham. Finally the day of departure arrived and after a big party I was farewelled at Manchester on the night mail train to London.

1966

London

Having family members living at Harrow in North London whom I had spent many of my school holidays with it was cheerios to them before getting myself to Heathrow airport and off to new horizons.

How was I to know the impact on my life the ten pounds I had spent on this venture to Australia was going to have? There I had been in Oldham, the only travelling to my name being a coach trip to the seaside now and again with my parents as a child growing up. Then as I approached my teenage years there were the school holidays at my aunt and uncle's house at Harrow. It was here I guess that the travel seed was planted. I would sometimes take the tube train into London with them and spend the days taking in the sights around the city. After leaving school at the end of 1954 there were no more travels until at age 19 I purchased my first of two motor bikes. They were both small ones being 125 cc, 2-stroke bikes. On these I was to take a look beyond the boundaries of Oldham on some weekend days, maybe Huddersfield or Burnley, other times Bury, Bolton or Rochdale, all 20 miles or so from home. From there I graduated to having a car at age 23. This brought on trips further afield with my group of now very close friends, many trips to watch Oldham Athletics away games, other times to follow Manchester United playing. Most times we would have two cars doing the trips with guys and girlfriends, and the girls would enjoy shopping in the towns we visited while we guys would be at the football match. Then along came 1965 and the ten pounds was spent to bring me to Sydney. Yes, how was I to know that 11 years hence I would have travelled more than 200,000 kilometres crossing 32 countries, the three major oceans and my life would change from what was essentially a home boy into what you are about read of in the following pages?

The aircraft was a Boeing 707 which would be taking me to Australia and I was pretty excited about the upcoming flight (my first ever) and the two years to follow. This was the amount of time that had to be spent in Australia to honour the subsidised fare of ten pounds. I was soon to find out that the Aussies referred to anyone English doing the trip on the scheme as a 'Ten Pound Pom'. I now realise nearly 50 years later sitting here in Tasmania, the island state of Australia that the saying will never change.

The journey itself was interesting, seeing the different cultures along the way. We disembarked at most of the refuelling stops. The flight path was via Zurich, Beirut, New Delhi, Singapore and Darwin which is where I had my first Aussie beer. It was very enjoyable and I did stretch it to having a second one! The biggest impact that I felt was at Singapore airport, nothing to do with people but to do with the heat. It was late evening, hot and humid with me in the clothes in which I had left London: winter woollen jumper, long trousers and more skins than an onion. Definitely not the right kind of clothing for the climate I found myself in. Hot and humid at 11pm!

Sydney, NEW SOUTH WALES

The aircraft arrived at Sydney airport at around 6am. My mate was there along with the family (mother and son our age) he was staying with in outer Sydney. We were driven to their home and after I had a shower and some breakfast it was decided to give me a 'Cooks Tour' of the city. However, sleep took over and the only thing I can remember of the drive was being told we were crossing the Sydney Harbour Bridge and seeing the large amount of steel with which it is built. That is etched in my memory even though I fell asleep again until arriving back at the house. Going straight to bed at around lunchtime I woke up at 10am the next day, having slept for about 22 hours or so. The first week was quite eventful, firstly getting some clothing to suit the conditions, secondly I got myself very sunburnt and thirdly my mate and I decided that outer Sydney was too far from the city so we moved into the city after only four days there.

On the third day I took myself into the city on the train network and took a bus to check out Bondi Beach. I had been into a clothes shop and got some shorts, t-shirts, socks and sneakers, I then took my English clothes to the left luggage at the railway station to pick up on the way back later. I foolishly went a bit overboard trying to get a tan on Bondi Beach with drastic results. The return trip on the train was broken to meet my mate in a pub by the station near his work after he had finished for the day. He took one look at me when I walked into the pub and asked what on earth I had done to myself. He reckoned I was in for a bad time with the sunburn. He was not wrong; we had been sitting at the bar in the pub for three or four beers when I decided a trip to the loo was called for. Another guy was in there already so I chose another place alongside him and he was most amused when I had to sink to my knees because the pain in my skin-shrunken legs was too much to bear while standing up. Without any doubt that was one of my most embarrassing moments!!

Taking the train to the city next day we found accommodation at a block of units on the north side of the Harbour Bridge at Kirribilli and arranged to move in there. The units were a three-storey newish building and on the first day there in the communal kitchen there was another guy cooking his dinner. He is still a close mate almost 50 years later. Also, at the same time as us moving in there another group of British guys had also moved in and one of them, a big strapping West Country bloke is also a close mate today. The accommodation block eventually became a source of socialisation with around 20 units in the building and with young males and females in residence making for a fun time. A communal lounge as well as kitchen made for good relationships among us there.

On the work front the first job I had was at a sugar processing factory. The job I was given was working around molasses tanks which had a terrible smell, and it was hot and sticky as well. This was not why I had come to the land of sunshine, to have a work situation like that, so I only stayed there for a week. Jobs in Sydney were plentiful in those days with the city expanding upwards as well as outwards at a fast rate. There were buildings being erected in many places around the city, it seemed, so I called into a new multi-storey site. After a short interview on site I was hired pretty much on the spot for the next day.

The work was on various kinds of wiring jobs on the building. That was fine but the company really wanted the employees to be chained to the mast, so to speak. I put up with it until one day the leading hand electrician came to me when I was working on a portable scaffold on the ground floor with a workmate who was from Townsville in Queensland. The leading hand asked me to run up to Level 14 where someone was needed. I told him I would walk up to the 14th (he did have others running by the way) and proceeded up there. After about an hour I went back down to continue where I had left off with my workmate. Within 10 minutes the site foreman came to the scaffold. The leading hand had complained to the boss that I would not follow orders and the foreman gave me my wage for the week along with my dismissal. He also gave me a week's pay extra because he had not agreed with the leading hand that I be given the sack for not doing as I was asked to do and run around the site. My workmate could not believe what was happening and told the foreman that if this was how things were with the company, then to bring his pay as well because he was out of there. He was the first of many fair dinkum Aussies I have come across over the years and really made me feel welcome in the country. I might add that the foreman was an Aussie but the leading hand was not, he was from Europe. I wondered if that made a difference.

Needing a job the next day I went over to the city and wandered onto the worksite of another multi-storey building not far from Circular Quay. There was a job available so I took the rest of the week off and started there the following Monday. I would travel across the Harbour Bridge on the train from one side to the other, from Milsons Point to Wynyard Station, which was just a stroll from the building in the city. It was on this job that I made my first major blue at work when I was delegated to fit power points onto the skirting ducts on the top three levels laid out as offices. That was fine as a lift was operating so I would take up three boxes of them after being in the crib room for my meal breaks. After a couple of days the leading hand came up to see how I was getting on with the job. It was then that I found out that Australian power points have the opposite pin configuration to the ones in Great Britain, and the ones I had fitted were all upside down. Oh dear, very embarrassing. The leading hand being an Aussie saw the funny side of it and was most amused when I explained the situation. All he said was that I was not in Pommy Land now. It was an easy task to retrace my steps and just turn them around anyway.

Chatting to the other electricians on the job I found out that the way to get top money along with food and accommodation was to get on what were called country jobs. That meant jobs in country towns or outback areas. After a week or two with that in mind, I approached the foreman with an inquiry towards getting out to any jobs available like that. The next day I was offered a transfer to a job in Wollongong about 50 miles down the coast from Sydney. A week later I was on a train.

Wollongong, NSW

Arriving at Wollongong I found my way to the hotel that the company had me booked into. It was almost opposite the railway station so that would be handy for getting the train back to Sydney for the weekends if I wanted to do that. I had been having a good social life in Sydney with the people from the units, with nights around the local hotels of North Sydney and also on Saturdays over at Manly, just a ferry ride across the harbour, for the beach and beer there. This, however, was Wollongong and I found myself working with unfamiliar materials which made the job quite interesting, if a little difficult at times. Much of the work involved welding and I had no experience at all with that. This led me into a difficult situation at another time which I will explain later. Somehow I managed to steer myself away from welding jobs with plenty of alternative tasks available.

The nightly activity here at Wollongong revolved around the bar at the pub, but I kept to myself on week nights, away from there. The guys drank much too fast for me! Probably ingrained from the days of the "6 o'clock swill", when all pubs had to close at 6 pm. Things became a bit more civilised with a 10 pm closure. The culture, however, might have been taking a while to change. I found myself going back to Sydney by train on Saturday mornings and returning on Sundays, so after three or four weeks I figured I may as well be living back there while making up my mind for my next change. Just for the record I managed to go the whole length of my 50 years as an electrician without having done any welding other than the situation that comes later.

10

Sydney, NSW

After arriving back at Sydney and having a few days' break from work I took a job from the multitude advertised for electricians in the Sydney Morning Herald, Saturday edition, with a city contractor. One of the jobs was on a new multi-storey building going up near Circular Quay. I was given the task of wiring in the Bundy clocks, with one installed on every level, controlled by a master clock in the top floor plant room. The building was some 15 storeys high with a service duct connecting all levels for the rising services of electrical and plumbing etc. Each level needed two wires from the master clock. To get the clocks wired, I figured that if I set up a rack of 30 cable drums on the top level and lowered the cables for them all to the bottom level through the spaces left in the concrete for the risers of different kinds, it would be easy to just alter the lengths as needed.

Great in theory! I set up the rack and taped a small weight on the end of the bunch and then commenced to lower the bunch of cables down into the duct. The wires were the smallest gauge of building wire so the 30 of them were no more than 50mm in diameter, easy to handle working alone. That was before I realised that the combined weight of the 30 wires was pretty heavy when on a downward travel with gravity helping them on their way. What a mess I ended up with! The cable drums just took off, spinning like crazy and did not stop until the 100 metre drums had unwound enough to have got me into a right old mess. When I went down the stairways to check the outcome I found a tangled mess on each level down to around Level 6 or so. Fate was a little kind to me as each cable did respond somewhat to being redrawn back up to the plant room after cutting the ends free below. There were enough trips up and down stairs untangling the mess to give me a good work out! It did take a fair chunk of the rest of the day to sort it out, and after that I took a lot more care when finishing the job!

After working on this site for a few weeks I decided to take off again to a country job. One was advertised as a short duration of three months in Tumut in the Snowy Mountains area of New South Wales so that looked interesting to me. After an interview I was booked on a flight down to Wagga Wagga and a bus to Adelong which was a real small town near Tumut. There was accommodation with the job at one of the three hotels in Adelong.

Adelong, NSW

On the flight to Wagga Wagga I was seated next to another English guy hailing from Birmingham. He was also an electrician on his way to the same job as me at Tumut. We were to become good travelling mates for the coming year or so along the east coast between Sydney in NSW and Cairns in Queensland. The job had been flooded with tradesmen to get the work done in a short time and the work was clean and situated in nice surroundings just on the outskirts of the town.

Adelong is a small town with a short main street which housed three pubs, the RSL Club and a few shops, and a population of just a few hundred people. The supervisor for the job here had organised for one of the electricians to give me a lift to the work site, around 20 kilometres from Adelong. He turned up next day, a young German guy with a ute with only one spare seat which was already taken. The only option for me was to sit in the cargo tray of the vehicle, alone!

Adelong and Tumut are not the warmest of places, especially at 6.30 in the morning in mid-autumn, and my first morning wash there is still memorable. No hot water at the sink and absolutely freezing cold water. Anyway, as for the ride to work I almost froze in the tray of the ute and I was very quick to rearrange another person to take me back at the end of the day in another car. Luckily, that night two more electricians arrived by car from Adelaide, so the other guy and I spent the rest of the time travelling with them to work. That in itself turned out to be an adrenalin boost each morning and afternoon, with the driver not seeming to know that the accelerator pedal has a space between stopped and flat out. His explanation was that he had been brought up on the gravel roads of South Australia and we would be quite safe as he knew no other way of driving a car except as fast as possible. He certainly lived by that code of driving behaviour. We were never late for work anyway even with one of the group dragging his feet every day to get ready for the ride.

The green hills surrounding Adelong, an old gold mining town, still had shafts down into the ground just wide enough for a man, sinking to a depth of over 100 feet. A stone dropped into these shafts took a number of seconds to hit the bottom. I explored these hills with great care at weekends. The shafts were unguarded and probably still are today, and if ever I should revisit them it will be with a great deal of caution.

There was a large construction project at this time nearby which was the Snowy Mountains Hydro-Electric Scheme. It was well in advance by now with dams being constructed throughout the area. The other two electricians who had joined us at the hotel suggested that our little group go to have a look at what was being done there. On one of the Sundays we hired a small aircraft from Tumut to take us on a scenic flight to see the scheme, and got to fly over the dams and lakes with power stations being built at various places. It was destiny for me to work at a couple of these sites in due course as well as taking a holiday at the ski fields which we also viewed on the flight. I have to admit to a bout of air sickness towards the end of the flight but I did manage to hold things together. Until then I had been fine, but the pilot decided to give us a look at the ski resorts close by. He flew the aircraft trailing some skiers along their ski run which meant many twists and turns, so it is little wonder that my stomach protested in a big way.

Another of the Sundays my now good mate and I took a walk to the gold fields for more exploring but this time we followed the bank of the creek that passed by the township on its way to a waterfall some way down the creek from there. The manager of the hotel had told us it was worth a visit so we took his advice. The creek was flowing quite fast but was not overly wide. We had not left to go walking until after lunch so I got to the stage where I thought it a bit late to continue that day as we still had a return walk to do. So we agreed to leave the walk to another day with more time to spend on it.

The creek had some rocks which I figured would be OK to use as stepping stones to get across to where the road into Adelong was in sight. Before my mate could stop me I was on my way across - yes I lost my footing on the wet rocks and into the creek I went. I soon found out how fast it was flowing with no chance of controlling my headlong rush forward in the current. The fact I am a non-swimmer did not really matter, the creek was in full control. Luckily, being able to fend myself off other rocks I could only think how far there was to go before the waterfall and how high it was. More luck when the current swirled me into a shallow pool on the opposite bank where I managed to get a footing. With a huge effort I was able to get myself onto the bank and then saw my mate running along the opposite bank towards me. He asked how I was to which I said I thought I was OK. He was not interested in trying to cross the creek himself which was decided with some laughter. We never did get to see the waterfall, as a return trip to see it did not happen. That wild ride down the creek is still etched in my memory however.

A very embarrassing moment occurred on a Friday night out in Adelong. There being not many places to go out, with just the three pubs and RSL club in the town a group of us electricians were having a few drinks in our hotel. As time progressed to around 8pm we heard music coming from across the road at the RSL club. The RSL is a club for returned servicemen from the armed forces of Australia and just about every town has one. We all trooped across the road and one of the members got us all signed in as visitors, about eight or nine of us. All went well until 9 pm when the lights went out. Quick as a flash with lightning humour I yelled out, "Is there an electrician in the house?"

My humour was short lived as one of our group gave me a quick jab in the ribs to shut me up but that was too late; the damage was done. As it was my first visit to an RSL club I did not know that every RSL in the country put the lights out and light a candle for the prayer offered to all the fallen servicemen in times of war. Of course, I realised my mistaken humour as soon as that happened and felt very foolish, which of course I had been. A couple of minutes later the lights came on again and the black looks came my way. A man approached me who probably was the president of the club and he asked me why such a disgraceful outburst. When I explained to him that it was my first time in an RSL club he saw that I had meant no disrespect and just told me that he hoped I had learned a lesson for any future visits. I had indeed done that!!

We had frequent visitors to the hotel from the closest of the Snowy Mountain Scheme sites at Talbingo. This was a small town which would be flooded over when the dams there were finished. There were three Italian workers who would come over for a few drinks, which always ended up with one of them in particular

15

drinking port wine straight from the bottle. That was fine except he was about 6 feet 6 inches tall and too big to argue with. He would throw his arms around your shoulders and say to you, "Drink" while holding his bottle to your mouth and pouring the stuff into you, all in good fun I might add. There were some good sing-songs on those nights.

One of the employees at the hotel lived at Talbingo and she told us that the town was due to be flooded over in two years' time. She sounded pretty sad about that, having always lived there and probably now in her 50s. There would be a new town to replace the one to be flooded so I guess that was a bright spot for those with homes there. It was in 1968 that I was to be working at the new town of Talbingo but more on that in later pages.

Another interesting day out was on a Sunday when, with three other guys from the site, I went to Canberra for a look around the capital city of the country. We went by car and the road trip through this part of the Snowy Mountains was particularly scenic. There was snow on the ground at a place called Kiandra where a couple of the guys got their first experience of being in snow. They were like a couple of young kids frolicking around in it. Eventually we continued on after making Kiandra a pit stop for a couple of beers and a bite to eat in the small tavern. When we got into Canberra it was nice to find a very clean, if rather quiet place, not many people out and about. A look at the Parliament House building and a most interesting tour around the Australian War Memorial just about filled in the rest of the day there. We did, however, find time for a meal in a nice Austrian restaurant before heading back to Adelong.

At the two month mark on the job things started to wind down, so my mate and I along with another electrician decided we would leave and do a road trip. He had a car and the plan was to head for the Gold Coast in Queensland. It had been good working here with an enjoyable party or two with the locals. I left Adelong first a few days before the others to spend a bit of time with my mates in Sydney before heading north.

ROAD TRIP TO QUEENSLAND

After I spent a week in Sydney the two mates from Adelong arrived and we set off pretty much right away. One of them had a brother who was living at Toukley about 60 kilometres north of Sydney. We spent a week at his flat which he shared with his girlfriend. It was overlooking the lake and a good place to relax for a while. There were many boats on the lake at night with lights hanging at the stern, which I found to be prawn boats out fishing. The nights were spent at the local hotel for drinks, or just chatting back at the flat. Development of the Central Coast of New South Wales was very much in its infancy at this time and has increased substantially since then.

After getting on the road again, a day's drive found us at the seaside town of Coffs Harbour in northern NSW. We set our tent up by the beach and after a meal we settled down to sleep. That was not to last for long because it turned out to be a wet and windy night. The tent lost its moorings and two of us 'slept' on the beach, while the other bloke was smugly in his car. We had the tent draped over the both of us in an effort to keep the rain off. The next day was much nicer so we spent most of the day there on the beach after which we travelled to the next little place we stayed at which was Yamba.

We found the beach to set up the tent again and lo and behold there was a RSL club close by! We had a meal there and a few drinks afterwards. Needless to say I was very careful to behave properly when 9 pm came around, making sure there was no repeat of the Adelong fiasco. Next day we got to the start of the Gold Coast at what are known as the twin towns of Tweed Heads and Coolangatta. The border between NSW and Queensland separates these two towns. We found a flat to rent a short way past Coolangatta close to the beach so we figured that it would be a good place to stay for a while.

Gold Coast, QLD

The flat we rented was in a resort complex and available for four weeks before the holiday season kicked in. We spent the time on the beach for the mornings when the weather was fine, which was most of the time, then lunch at the pub, The Cabbage Patch, in Coolangatta. That was pretty much the way the days' activities for the following three months or so panned out here on the Gold Coast. At the three week mark we had found a three bedroom house to rent at Palm Beach, a little further along the coast and would you believe, the rent was 25 dollars each per week. Our local pub became the hotel at Burleigh Heads, with much time spent on the nearby beach.

At the beach promenade there was a young guy who had set himself up with a tank of suntan oil, a compressor of some sort and it was all a package kept on an old butcher's bicycle. He was seated comfortably on a chair and had a sign advertising all-over body suntan oil sprays for 50 cents. He had no shortage of takers and had set himself up with a very worthwhile occupation. Would you believe that when I was to return to Burleigh Heads while on a Gold Coast family holiday 27 years later with my wife and four children there was still a guy there doing the same job, albeit not from a butcher's bike. He was as brown as a berry and skin

18

somewhat wrinkled. Maybe the same guy. I should have asked him. That just went to prove that there was opportunity here in Australia. The three of us stayed at Palm Beach until about the middle of November before moving again into a small apartment in Surfers Paradise, another move in a northerly direction along the coast.

The township of Surfers Paradise was little more than a small town then, with the only multi-storey building in use from memory being No 10 The Esplanade, overlooking the beach. We were to spend most of our nights locally but there was one night that the three of us made a return trip to Coolangatta for a night out in The Cabbage Patch pub there. Luckily there was a cabaret that night with good music and dancing on the small dance floor. At around 8.30 a group of females walked into the room, all looking blonde and gorgeous. When the music for dancing began to play the three of us were over to their table like bees around a honey pot asking three of them for a dance. I guess we did that two or three more times and each time got knocked back. After an hour or so the MC announced on the stage an important piece of news for their patrons, that the hotel would soon be hosting a regular floor show featuring the Les Girls Female Impersonating Troupe and they were in the hotel for the evening to be introduced to all there. They were to set up a regular feature due to commence shortly. It is probably obvious what had happened, yes we had been completely taken in by the girls who were of course, the boys. No more dancing for the three of us that night I can say. Another of those moments when I got embarrassed for a moment or two!

The days at Surfers were spent pretty much the same as before with things revolving around the beach, the two pubs, and generally relaxing. Seeking employment did start to cross our minds as we could not keep on with this lifestyle forever. Money would soon start to play a part. The two pubs at Surfers were the Surfers

Paradise Hotel at the centre of town and the Chevron Hotel nearby. The Surfers Hotel on the corner of Caville Avenue and the highway did a one dollar (including salad) barbecue lunch in the beer garden, which also had a swimming pool. This was our lunch on most days.

There was one day here that we drove into Brisbane to check the city out. Brisbane at this time was known as Australia's biggest country town, with no high-rise buildings to speak of and with the residential areas spread far and wide. Along the road we passed through bushland at Beenleigh with building blocks of land advertised for sale for $750. That area now is inundated with people and built up to the extreme with the city of Logan close by. The price for building blocks would now be far in excess of $750. An opportunity lost, one could say. The only building I can remember seeing of any significance back then was the Rum Distillery at Beenleigh.

As time moved on towards Christmas the money factor came into the equation so we all three decided it was time to move on. We got a Courier Mail Saturday newspaper and the ads in there for electricians were just as plentiful as they were in the Sydney newspaper. We stayed at Surfers for Christmas, then it was on with the thinking caps for what to do next.

We decided to drive up to Maryborough where a shipyard was advertising for tradesmen to work on a new boat-building contract. We arrived there at the end of December.

1967

Maryborough, QLD

We spent a couple of days here seeing in the New Year, enjoying New Year's Eve at a beachside hotel at Torquay which was recommended. It was worth the drive over, for a good night's entertainment. To cut a long story short, I awoke the next morning in a picnic shelter at Torquay. At least I was out of the rain. Starting back to Maryborough on foot, I was lucky to be picked up by a ute. More than lucky actually, as the road was covered in water much of the way. Back at the hotel, I found my mates still in bed, having given me up for lost.

The three of us went together to the shipyard when they reopened and after a look around with the personnel manager I decided against working there. The work would be very hot, inside either the workshops or the boats being built. My mate with the car, however, decided to accept a start, as it turned out he had made a date to see a female. My other mate and I kept heading north by bus to Gladstone.

Gladstone, QLD

We went directly to the Commonwealth Employment Service (CES) and both took jobs on a new power station being built near the town of Biloela. We booked into a hotel in Gladstone for the night ready to get a bus to Biloela the next day from where we would be transported to the site.

The night at the hotel in Gladstone was not without a bit of excitement as I had my first encounter with the huge insects that abound in Queensland. There was a mosquito net above each of the beds in our room and after I got into my bed I decided it would be a good idea to lower it down for the night. As I did this a huge insect dropped out of it and I hit the panic button trying my best to both get out of the bed while draped in the net and attack the creature not knowing how dangerous it might be. My mate, seeing the commotion, dashed over and raised the net allowing me to get on my feet on the floor. The thing flew onto a picture rail while all I could hear was raucous laughter at my reaction to a harmless stick insect, the biggest insect I had ever seen. They sure do have big ones here, compared to home!

Biloela, QLD

At Biloela we were met by a man from the company we were to work for and taken to the construction camp where we were given a cabin each and bedding, then shown around the camp. It was not very big with just the cabins and a mess for taking meals in. There was also a block with showers and toilets. The power station we would be working on was a pretty small one and at the time of writing this, from looking at a recent trade magazine I found out that it was decommissioned some time ago. Thinking of the work that we did there I wonder what has happened to all the copper cable that would have been in the ground. Explaining about that, the job that we were given was working as a pair, installing the earthing mat around the power station. This was made up of large diameter stranded cable, set in a chequerboard pattern in trenches already dug and then brazed together at all the crossover points. So there was a very large quantity of copper in the ground at a depth of 600mm, and I think it would have been well worth the effort of salvage after decommissioning.

Our site supervisor was the kind of bloke who made sure all of the electricians gave their pound of flesh at work. There were about eight others besides the two of us and I was given the job of going around the site in the truck to pick them all up for lunches in the mess. Woe betide me if I collected the supervisor (who was to be the last pick up) more than a couple of minutes before the break. Keeping to the times for work has to be observed of course, but a little bit of flexibility would have been appreciated.

We went into Biloela one night for a few beers and a bloke at the bar there was from the Moura coal mine which was just being made into the giant of a place it is now. He was an electrical foreman there and he set about asking if we might be interested in a job there. He said he had a chain in his car boot and would tie us to the post outside and pick us up in the morning if we were keen. In all seriousness jobs then were that easy to get.

The instance that saw us move on from the job at the power station was the day that my mate came over to where I was working and asked me to give him a hand to get some more cable with the truck from the compound where it was stored. We had been told by the leading hand to work independently but to help each other with anything that was too hard for one person. We had got to the compound and unrolled 25 metres of the cable from a cable drum and rolled it up ready to lift onto the truck. We had lifted it into position to heave it up into the truck's tray when in came the supervisor. He wanted to know why we were both doing the job when he believed it should be a job for one person. My mate came back at him with justification that the sheer weight of the roll of cable was far too much for one to handle. The upshot was that he told the supervisor that this was not a good attitude and that he would quit. The supervisor turned to me and said that he supposed the same would go for me to which I replied in the affirmative. We worked two days' notice during which time we got a Courier Mail newspaper and secured a job from that. Just a phone call to Brisbane was enough.

We were told to go to Mt Morgan where we would be booked into The Golden Nugget Hotel. We were to wait for someone from the company who would arrive over the weekend. The job was an extension to the hospital there. Being a Friday when we travelled to the new job it made for a good weekend with work not starting until the Monday. After a bus ride from Biloela we found The Golden Nugget Hotel and waited there as we were asked. The publicans made us welcome and seemed happy when they were told we did not know how long we would be staying with them until the guy from Brisbane turned up.

Mt Morgan, QLD

On Sunday afternoon the electrician from Brisbane arrived with all the paperwork for the two of us to fill in to be formally employed. It was here that I found out that the licence system for electricians in Australia was very disjointed. The work I had been doing in NSW was as an unlicensed electrician because I had not done any examinations yet for a full licence anywhere since arriving in the country. However, in NSW that was allowed so long as a fully licenced electrician was in charge of the job. This was all news to me.

This meant that I had to apply for a permit from the licensing board in Brisbane to work in Queensland. The permit would last for three months and then I would have to sit an examination. An alternative was that my employer could vouch for me in order for me to be granted a licence without an examination after the three months had elapsed. That was what eventually happened at Mt Morgan, with a favourable report from my employer.

The work started on the Monday morning and one of the first people I came across was another Pom from St Helens near Liverpool. He was a bloke about 60 years of age and when I asked him how long he had been in Australia he told me he had been over here for 42 years. I never in my wildest dreams would have expected to surpass that, but I have outdone any expectation by going well beyond that, albeit having been on and off a bit!

The hotel was a very old one, same as a lot of the hotels, especially in the country towns. The publican was an Italian by name but with an Aussie accent and most likely a second generation Aussie. He was running the place with his wife and a young son. We were to stay there for about four months and I really found myself feeling like one of the family by the time the job was done. The publican happened to be the head coach of the two local soccer teams, Mt Morgan 1 and Mt Morgan 2. He was quick to assume that being English we must play football and he hoped we would give it a go to play for one of the teams. We did just that and were put in the team for the next Sunday with Mt Morgan 2 after a couple of nights training at the town oval. The games were played in Rockhampton where all teams on the roster played on a Sunday. There was a sports ground for football where all the teams would meet to get through the roster for the week. The result of that match escapes me but we did play a game or two while there.

The Easter holiday long weekend came and it turned out to be pretty eventful. There had been a change of leading hands on the job with the new one having a house at Yeppoon just out of Rockhampton on the coast. He said that we should take a tent there and camp at the local camping ground for the holiday, and we were also invited to dinner with him and his wife for Easter

Sunday. The leading hand had a yacht and he sailed with a yacht club along the coast from Yeppoon. He had asked us if we would act as crew for him in a yacht race around one of the Keppel Islands which are offshore of Yeppoon. My mate agreed but I declined because I am a non-swimmer but that was OK as there was a mate of the leading hand to make up the crew of three. The race was set down for Easter Sunday morning. We went to Yeppoon with him in his car and set up at the camping ground on the Thursday after work.

When we got back to the tent after visiting the hotel on Saturday night we were just getting into our sleeping bags when my mate started carrying on about a flying insect in his eye. It left him in a sorry state and in a bit of pain from it. He felt it was bad enough to get some attention to it so we went around to the site manager who gave us directions to find the local hospital to have someone take a look at it. The result was that he was kept in there for the night so I went back to the camp. I took myself over to the hospital next morning to find him just about ready to leave, with a huge dressing covering the eye. He told me that we had better go to the house to let the leading hand know there was a problem for doing the crew job for him. He asked if I would take my mate's place in the crew. After a lot of discussion of for and against I was finally convinced to do it as I would have a life jacket and a rescue boat followed the race for any emergencies. In fact my mate was delegated to assist in the rescue boat and it was needed!

The yacht was a 13 foot racing yacht and I was given instructions on how to go from one side of the boat to the other without getting hit by the boom as it swung when changing tack. My job was to hang over the side as counterbalance which I seem to remember was called 'on the trapeze'. It was, much to my amazement, a very enjoyable experience being my first time sailing. I was managing the crossovers without being hit by the boom and the silence out on the water was really good, with just the sound of the hull slapping down on the water now and again.

We were about halfway out to Big Keppel Island when things took a turn for the worst. A sound like a whiplash rang out and one of the stays from below the deck to the top of the mast tried its best to pull through the deck which was made of fibreglass, or was that plywood? I lost track of what went on with the other two crew - they were the experienced pair after all. All I remember is being told not to worry as we would turn around and head back to shore. That was OK until one of them said that we could lose the mast at any time. Doing my best to keep calm, I just followed instructions as they came. We had managed to get on course for the shore when who should turn up in the rescue boat but my mate. He was not very sympathetic, making fun of the situation while following us back to shore. We did make it and a couple of drinks or so in the yacht club were very welcome when we had got things sorted with the damaged boat.

It was a short time after that when our road trip mate from Maryborough made a trip to Mt Morgan to catch up. He decided he would finish up on the job down there and join us at the hospital job. It would have been the long weekend in June when the three of us decided to visit Emerald where we could fossick for gemstones. After we organised our official miners' rights we set off on the Friday after work. We now had the car so we were able to get to the area easily. On the Saturday we had a look around Emerald, the only town of any size out there near the diggings. We then continued on out to the areas of Sapphire and Ruby Vale. There was plenty of digging going on with camps set up mainly using caravans for shelter and sleeping. We had the tent which accommodated three and set that up when we were able to find what was to be our claim, 100 yards x 100 yards as I remember. We had to check with neighbouring claims that we were not claim-jumping and soon realised things were taken very seriously in that regard. In fact we were to spend more time talking to the miners there than doing any digging if the truth be known.

There were lots of old guys with stories to tell. One of them told us how to come by water when we asked him how to get some and where from. He told us that there was a council bore pump at Sapphire, a small settlement near to us but the water was very brackish and not very nice to drink. He went on to say that there was however, a guy with a camp set up with his own bore pump and the water from that was much nicer to the taste. The bloke did charge for the water but was reasonable. We got directions to this camp which turned out to be just a short 10 minute walk from ours. We collected our billy cans and a couple of drink bottles that we had and made our way. He was more than happy to supply us with the water and when he spoke I recognised an accent from the north of England. It turned out that he was from Ashton which is only a short way from Oldham, probably no more than 10 kilometres apart! As we were only there for a few days he said for us to come over any time we needed more water, and there would be no charge. We had a chat with him for a while and he told us that most of the guys there were older people just keeping busy and some were lucky enough to make some cash for their efforts. He said that a young couple had been to do the same as what we were doing a short time ago and found a sapphire worth at least $1000 so that gave us some encouragement. But it was not to be, as it turned out. A very interesting few days anyway, before going back to work at Mt Morgan.

We spent most of our Saturday nights at a small township called Bouldercombe on the road to Rockhampton; it was always a good time there. Along with a few houses there was a pub and a hall, and a dance was usually held in the hall with a four-piece band providing the music. The pub close by was used for refreshment. It was good to mix with the locals there. Our mate from Maryborough did not stay very long at Mt Morgan and was soon to return to Maryborough to meet up again with his girlfriend there. That was the last I saw of him so what happened to him after that is an unknown. My mate and I were to move on as well soon after that when the job was just about finished.

The time spent at The Golden Nugget pub had been very enjoyable and we made friends with many guys around the bar and also the waitress staff. It was good to be moving on to somewhere different but the pub and its locals will always be remembered for happy times. The publican gave us a lift to Rockhampton to catch a train to Cairns in Far North Queensland.

While working here at Mt Morgan I realised that the idea of Australia being the land of opportunity was really true. Finding work whenever I tried was so easy with good paying jobs in what seemed to be an endless supply. I made a promise to myself to work my way around the country making time to enjoy my surroundings while doing it.

Cairns, QLD

After a long train ride to Cairns mainly passing sugar cane plantation after plantation we arrived there to be greeted with high temperatures and high humidity, a far cry from what I had so far experienced in my stay in Aussie. There was a nice motel where we were to stay for a few days in the city centre. When the sun started to go down and the day started to turn into night it became very much nicer to be out in the cool of the evening. Completely the opposite to the daytime, it was really pleasant to be outside. Especially at twilight, I can almost still hear the sounds of the insects chirping and warbling as well as the frogs croaking all over the place. I have since realised that it would have been the cane toad population making themselves heard, since they are now a designated pest.

As it happened, we stayed in Cairns for about four days and during this time visited what was called a beach bordering the city centre but looked more like a grey mudflat. One night we made a visit to the cinema and that was a surprise waiting for me. We bought the tickets at a small foyer at the front of the cinema and then proceeded through a door into the auditorium only to find ourselves outside again. It was an open air cinema but very nice to be out in the cool air. There was cover over the rear of the seating which was underneath what must have been the dress circle seats and maybe this area had a roof over it for cover. Whatever the case may be I guess with rain and wind direction it would be a gamble taking the front seats up or under. The experience was worthwhile but the metal deckchairs did lack in a little comfort.

Another trip we had was on a ferry over to Green Island which is a coral cay about 15 kilometres offshore from Cairns and forms part of the Great Barrier Reef. The sea on the way over was the deepest blue I have *ever* seen! There was just a bar on the island for drinks and snacks, and glass bottom boats to look at the underwater coral and the fish swimming around, very colourful. Snorkelling and swimming looked really good for the ones doing that and I wished I could swim to get down there with a snorkel for a proper look. That is one regret that I have which keeps popping up.

After we had spent the few days here we felt it was time to move so we booked seats on a train to Brisbane. My mate decided he would get a flight to New Zealand from there and then go back to England one way or another, so Brisbane was where we were to part company. It had been a good year or so, we had been good mates and I did catch up with him again about two years later on my first trip back to England, visiting him and his family while there. I found out then that he had got married and now was a family man with a baby girl so that was a nice thing to find.

Arriving in Brisbane we had a good night out and the following day I booked the bus to Sydney back in NSW, to catch up once again with my friends there.

Sydney, NSW

When I got to Sydney my mates there were all still living at the same place in Kirribilli so I had found myself a place to bed down. I struck lucky with that as I did not intend staying in Sydney for too long because I was eager to start a trip around the country. When I found out that one of them was thinking of going for a skiing holiday to Thredbo Village in the Snowy Mountains this appealed to me. We decided it would be good to do a holiday like that together and made the arrangements. This meant there would be return flights to Cooma and transport from there to the village. The mate who had the idea for the trip had grown up at Cooma and was able to ski well while I would be a complete learner but looking forward to it. It made sense to get a job for a couple of weeks in the city to fill in the time before going so I found one on a renovation of a huge house, working with two other electricians for a city contractor. I guess the money I earned from that paid for the holiday.

It was good to catch up with my mate from home again who told me that he had been away working in New Guinea but had needed to return to Sydney, because of an injury he had at work which had developed a tropical ulcer that would not heal in the tropics.

Cooma, NSW

Arriving at Cooma we were met by a shuttle bus which took us to the village. The accommodation was in the village hotel and the ski fields were virtually on the door step. We had a great time there with many a slip and a fall on the skis but by the end of the holiday there I had learned the basics and was able to tackle the slopes for intermediate skiers. There were two old friends of my mate from his Cooma days who worked at the resort on the weekends. They had told us that we should catch up with them when leaving Cooma for a beer or two at a pub there. We arranged this for the day of our flight back to Sydney. Our departure was scheduled for 5.30 pm, so plenty of time for a drink. That was the plan; however, some plans do not run true to course.

We met the two guys at a pub and there was a third guy there as well; it turned out that all three had grown up with my mate and all of them went to the same school as kids. Anyway we had a good afternoon with them and finally I noticed the time was 5.15! Too late to make the plane so I used the phone at the pub to call the airline to explain that we would not be able to get to the flight on time. This is where our luck came in because the consultant just said not to worry as there was a flight to Sydney with vacant seats for us the next day, and to turn up at the airport for our new tickets then. Could it be imagined - that sort of thing happening today? No chance, I reckon. We ended up having tea at one of his mates houses and then making our way back to town to find beds for the night. Not an easy thing to do in Cooma on a Saturday night but we did eventually. We also managed to make it to the airport on time the next day.

Back in Sydney I decided to continue travelling south on my way to circle the country before my two years were up. I booked a seat on a bus to Melbourne and left a couple of days later.

Melbourne, VICTORIA

My stay in Melbourne was very brief. After booking into a hotel in the city and looking around the city centre I checked out the work situation knowing that the electrical licence system in Australia is different for every state. So far I had been able to work without a licence in NSW, I now had a licence to work in Queensland but in Victoria I was about to find out it was harder to get permission for work without a Victorian licence. I was told by the licencing board that it was necessary to find a job before any steps could be taken to get a licence in any form. I did not want to get tied up in any red tape at this stage so I decided to move on to Adelaide in South Australia, where they had the same set up as in NSW. I did have three or four days in Melbourne just to get the feel of the city. I was to get to know Melbourne much better a few years down the track, however. A bus to Adelaide in South Australia then was my next move.

Adelaide, SOUTH AUSTRALIA

Arriving in Adelaide I once again did my usual thing and booked into a hostel in the city centre. After a stroll around I went into a hotel bar for a quiet beer and there got chatting to three other guys. They were English soccer players in the city for the weekend to play in a competition and were from Whyalla, a town out along the coast to the west. They had told me that work was easy to get there at the steelworks, especially for tradesmen. Having had intentions of making Perth in Western Australia my next stop it seemed to me that it would be a good stepping stone along the way.

That weekend an Australian Rules football match was being played in Adelaide on the Saturday afternoon, so I found my way to the Adelaide Oval where Sturt were to play North Adelaide. I had not seen an Aussie Rules match yet so reckoned it would be a good opportunity to put that right. Having been brought up on Football, (Soccer to the Aussies), and Rugby League I did not have a clue of the rules or scoring of Aussie Rules football. The match turned out to be very one sided on the score board and at the end of the third quarter it was obvious that the team in front would be easy winners. I had not really liked the game anyway, still having the round ball game of football in my blood. I decided to beat the rush out of the ground and go back into the city centre for a beer or two before the pubs shut for the day. This was still the time of 6 o'clock closing of pubs in South Australia so that would take a bit of getting used to. In the course of time I did get to like the game of footy but my first look at it was not encouraging. I am now a fan of the football team St Kilda in Melbourne who actually won the Victorian Football League Grand Final of 1966, the year I arrived in Australia. They are still waiting to win another one almost 50 years later. Everything comes to those who wait, so they say!

Although my stay in Adelaide was a brief one the city made a good impression on me as a nice quiet place and very clean. It would have been good to get to know it a bit better but the opportunity that I had been given was too good to miss. So I headed west on buses to Whyalla via Port Augusta.

Whyalla, SA

I stayed overnight in a town centre pub, and felt it best to take a look around the town before making my next move. Whyalla was not a very large town so it did not take very long. Next morning I went to the steelworks to check out the work situation. The guys were correct in saying that I would get a job there. I got an interview on the spot, and started work the next day. Whyalla is right on the coast so I figured that a stay here for a while should be OK.

The work was similar to what I had been doing on the power station near Biloela, involving installation of an earthing mat. The ground was rock hard and my job was to insert earthing rods of about four feet in length, with the help of a jack hammer. Not an easy task but certainly something different for me to be doing. There was a fair bit of sweat from my brow along the way. I was allocated a room for accommodation at one of the company's hostels, where there was a canteen for meals as well as cut lunches to take to work. These were in the factory grounds so there was only the walk to and from work from my hostel every day. The cost for the boarding was taken out of my pay and was very cheap, not free as with the other country jobs I had worked at but being in a town I guess that was a fair thing. From the camp to the town was just walking distance so any activities there were in easy reach. The social life here was a bit limited with not having a pub to visit after 6 o'clock but a social club near to the hostel, again run by the company did provide an outlet for some socialising. I joined in with some other blokes there mainly for card games and darts.

Fridays after work we were regulars at one of the pubs in town for a quick beer or two before 6 o'clock raised its ugly head. It soon became apparent that raffles were popular on these evenings with prizes of meat trays, chickens or fish. One of them I actually managed to win with the prize being a huge fish. Not a real lot I could do with that as I got my meals at the hostel, so I gave it to one of my workmates who I was with because he had a family at home where it would be of better use. I soon learnt that these 'Chook Raffles' are common in pubs with a chook being a chicken here in Aussie. The Sunday afternoons turned out to be OK as

35

well. The guys who had told me about Whyalla played soccer with The Wanderers club so I would go there for an hour or two and watch the football (soccer), and have a few drinks when the games were played. After a few weeks here I reckoned on not staying any longer as I was keen to keep moving, so I departed Whyalla to go to Port Augusta and link up with the train to Perth in Western Australia.

Train to Perth, Western Australia

Across the Nullarbor Plain was a very long train ride across wide open country with no vegetation other than small stubby bushes growing in the red earth for a distance of about 2000 kilometres. There were four or five small settlements along the line through the Nullarbor which served as homes for the maintenance people who worked on the line. The train was used to supply them and their families with their essential supplies as well as carrying the passengers and freight. It made stops at the settlements where a small group of residents would come aboard to collect items. These settlements were few and far between with large expanses of the plain to cross from one to the next.

There was no one sharing the accommodation with me on the train so I was sleeping well. The train had a club car on it for socialising with other passengers so that was good too. The view outside did not change much, if at all, for the major part of the ride to Kalgoorlie. Consequently the club car got quite a bit of use.

The train did not go direct to Perth at this time and there had to be a change of trains at Kalgoorlie. This was because of a different track gauge laid for the rest of the journey. The carriage I was in for this trip was very old and a delight to see. All polished timber and with brass fittings complementing that, I hope it has found its way into a railway museum now that the Indian Pacific train does the journey from Sydney to Perth and return without having to change trains at Kalgoorlie these days.

Perth, WA

By now I was into a routine when arriving in a different state. I would first find accommodation and then find out what there might be to do around the area for some good entertainment. The next thing would be checking where the Electrical Licencing Board was, to check what was needed by them to get a job. In Western Australia it was a requirement to obtain a permit, using documentary evidence that allowed you to work for six months, then an exam had to be done to get a full licence. After a few days to have a good look at the city and get a feel for it I got a permit organised for working after looking at the job adverts in the Saturday newspaper. Heaps of jobs once again for electricians. I figured the country jobs would be best if I wanted to see Aussie in its raw state so to speak, so I applied for and got a job at an iron ore mine in the Pilbara region of the state up in the North West. This was the Mt Goldsworthy mine and it was about 100 kilometres east of Port Hedland. The company had an office in Perth so I was able to get it all sorted out there before being flown up to Port Hedland and met there for the trip to the mine site in a company bus.

Mt Goldsworthy, WA

Port Hedland is around 1600 kilometres north of Perth, with Mt Goldsworthy mine site a further 100 kilometres inland, so it took just about all day for the trip. The heat that struck me as I got off the aeroplane at Port Hedland was something I was going to have to get used to. That was easier said than done and it was a good three weeks before I was even close to it. I was met by the company bus, a dust-encrusted vehicle, with all of the windows wide open for some necessary ventilation. The mine was still in the developmental stage, only having been started the previous year, so the road to the mine was unsealed as yet which meant that dust thrown up by the bus was blown into the inside of the bus making it a very unpleasant ride. Even though it was late afternoon by now the heat was something to be reckoned with. As I looked at the surrounding countryside while riding on the bus my first thoughts were that it must look like this on the moon, tinder-dry red earth as far as the eye could see in all directions. I had told myself that I wanted to see Australia in its raw state, and I reckon that was what was happening now.

Arriving at the township which was being built to service the mine I was allocated a room and shown where the mess hall was. There was also an old railway carriage which had been stripped and converted to serve as a bar for the use of the workers to have a beer or two. I made use of that after having had a meal even if only to wash away the dust from my throat following the bus ride. It was the end of winter when I started work here and I was to stay for a couple of months until November as it turned out. Once again the social life was a bit limited. With only the railway carriage for socialising, there was not a real lot of opportunity for that with working 10 hour days. The upside was plenty of overtime at work, a good opportunity for saving for what would be coming afterwards. That really set in place the way I was to spend the next 10 years or so, saving hard on mining or construction projects then travelling to enjoy the fruits of all the work.

Soon after starting work I was paired up with another electrician who was from Yugoslavia. We were working on the lighting around a couple of large bins which were to be used as ore bins. It meant welding brackets around the outside for the lights so the other guy asked me to weld them onto the bin while he started running cables. I had never done any welding before but had seen it done often enough. I figured it should be easy enough to do, so just got on with it. I was managing OK or so I thought. I had three or four done when an almighty bellow went out from my Yugoslav mate. He had used one as a support for his foot while up his ladder and when he had put his weight on the bracket it had snapped off and he all but took a tumble. I might add he was about 6 foot 2 and a very large man who was far from amused. Needless to say we swapped jobs after that. This was probably the catalyst for my non-welding career to follow!

The next job was to start work on installing some lights around what was to be a bowling green. Nothing on Earth could look nothing more like a bowling green than this patch of bone dry red earth did right then. We had to dig a trench for laying cables as well as deep holes for the concrete pads where the light poles would be. I was given a pick and shovel and set to work. The ground was hard as concrete and made up of what I could only describe as small layered flat rocks, just about impossible with the tools I was given to dig a trench with, let alone deep holes as well. I told the foreman that a back hoe was needed to do the job so that was as far as I got with that one. Not sorry either as with starting work at 7 am after having breakfast and the 10 hour working day ahead with the sun just starting to warm up, to say the place was unpleasant was only a starting point. By 8 am it was almost unbearable heat out in the glare of the sun. It was little wonder that I was not sorry to see that job halted for a while.

I was then given jobs around the town site which suited me fine. After a couple of weeks another new starter arrived who somehow or other got paired as a work mate with me and there were a couple of unusual incidents to follow. One concerned work when we were given the job of monitoring the water usage for the township. At this time the township consisted of a number of single men's accommodation blocks with the toilets and shower cubicles for them in another building and about a dozen or so houses already built and lived in. As for purchasing everyday items there was a shop there which covered that. It also served as a milk bar with take away food prepared there as well. There was a block of relocatable offices for administration and not much else so that was the town of Goldsworthy for the moment.

The job for us to do was at a water bore just out of the town, which had a pump drawing water from underground. The two of us were to measure the water level down the bore hole by dropping a stone down it and timing how long before it hit the water. This was done every 30 minutes for ten hours a day for seven days. The boss told us to take books with us so as not to get too bored with the job. We were to take drinking water and have meal breaks separately. A shelter was set up for some shade otherwise I reckon we would have ended up cooked with the constant sunshine and heat. It was good that there were the two of us otherwise I reckon we might have gone crazy doing that job alone. My workmate and I were both of the same opinion that electricians would not be doing this as part of their job where we came from. He was from France.

Another episode was when he and I were working on a job in the township which had become the normal day's work for us. I saw a large delivery truck with the driver unloading armful after

40

armful of artificial flowers at one of the houses. The truck had come from one of the big department stores in Perth and the lady of the house began planting them in the hard, dry ground around the garden. The ground was hard as concrete, knowing that from my efforts when I was on the bowling green job. Anyway the lady persevered and she finished up with a very colourful garden at her house. She had certainly brightened the garden and she got points from me for trying but really went to extremes for the result.

In November I decided it was time to move on as it was only three more months before the two years would be over for what was my intended time to experience Australia. A full circular trip around the country was my objective (I had not considered Tasmania at this time). Therefore, I got the daily bus back to Port Hedland for another look at the lunar landscape on the way. I spent a couple of days in Port Hedland to sort out my banking and top up on my clothing which had diminished somewhat. I did a tour around the hotels, all three of them as I recall with very little else to do in the town. Back in the 60s development was a key word for many towns and Port Hedland fitted the bill in that regard.

There was a flight to Darwin to follow with drop-offs and pick-ups at Derby, Broome and Wyndham on the way.

Darwin, NORTHERN TERRITORY

Arriving in Darwin in mid-afternoon I found a clean-looking guest house in the city centre which would be handy for exploring from. After a walk around I found Darwin to be much more humid than the Pilbara. These huge differences in climate during my trip around Australia became a feature for me. After having a meal I decided on an early night. The guest house was a pretty old building and my room was up a couple of flights of stairs with a small balcony looking out towards the sea a short distance away. When night fell the thunder and lightning started, but no rain. I sat out on the balcony to watch the light show that nature was providing. An electrical storm was going on and the sight was just mind-blowing, flash after flash, one after another in rapid succession. It was not just solo flashes on many occasions but multiple flashes. Something I will never forget for sure, the streaks were literally slashing across the sky and some piercing down towards the sea. Then came the rain and talk about heavy rain, just huge raindrops and plenty of them. My first experience of a tropical storm is etched in my memory forever. There have been more to follow in later years but that night in Darwin is the one that gives me this lasting memory.

With the weather in Darwin at this time of year being very hot and humid during the day I did not look forward to having to work in this climate so decided to just spend the week there and then travel back to Sydney by bus. That was the plan anyway. I set it in motion by booking a bus ticket to Brisbane via Tennant Creek, Townsville and then on to Brisbane. It was my intention to spend a few days there and the Gold Coast before travelling back to Sydney.

I boarded the bus which took me south to the Three Ways, a T-junction on the highway just north of Tennant Creek, then east to Mount Isa in Queensland, prepared for a long ride. Everything went well through Katherine and the short break at Daly Waters. The huge termite mounds which abound in the bush on this part of the journey were the main feature. The bus from Three Ways was where the plan started to come a little bit unstuck. It was a trip of about 650 kilometres from Three Ways to Mount Isa and we were about 100 kilometres from Mount Isa when the bus decided it was time for a rest. The engine just died and we were broken down. The driver had a look for the problem but was unable to do anything about getting the engine to restart. It was somewhere around lunchtime and pretty hot with the air conditioning now not working. The driver decided the best plan would be for him to get a lift when someone was passing and get some help from Mount Isa. The highway was not sealed at this time and passing traffic was a bit of a luxury. Anyway, someone did come along and gave the driver a lift. I guess by now it was somewhere between 1.30 and 2.00 pm. The other eight or so passengers and I battened down in the bus to wait. Time just went on and on and with mobile phones yet to make their impact on people's lives, waiting was our only option other than trying to hitch a ride. So we waited and waited until at about the three hour mark a four wheel drive wagon pulled up behind the bus.

The driver was from a cattle station nearby and he had seen the bus from his property, wondering why it was there for such a long time. He said he would go back to his home and try to find out what was happening in Mount Isa. He came back about half an hour later with the news that the company who ran the service had no idea what had happened and were themselves worried that the bus had not arrived at the depot. They had asked the driver of the wagon if he could tow us on to his property until next day when a relief bus would be sent out to pick us up, and a mechanic to work on our bus.

We were towed onto the station and the owner really turned on the hospitality. A barbecue was set up along with a camp fire by some of his jackaroo workers there, the guitars came out and a good old sing song developed with plenty of food and drink for everyone. We were able to sleep on the bus and enjoyed a good breakfast by the camp fire next day before the relief bus turned up. I got into Mount Isa and later that day found a motel for the night before moving on. It seemed like a good idea to spend a couple of days here first.

Mount Isa, QUEENSLAND

Very hot here so the first thing to do was check out the three pubs that formed three corners of the main shopping block of the city. It still seems quite funny to me how a place with such a small area of shops can be designated a city. What's more, the area of land that makes up the city is about 43,000 square kilometres, which is larger than some countries! It is literally in the middle of nowhere as the saying goes. A trip to Google shows just how isolated it is.

That aside however, I got chatting to a guy in one of the pubs and once again was told that jobs were easy to get at the mine here if I was interested. The climate here was very different to Darwin with a similar heat factor but little or no humidity, making it a dry heat. So after visiting the bus depot to arrange a stopover here I made my way to the mine which formed part of the city's infrastructure and lo and behold got a job easy as that. Accommodation was a single room at the single men's quarters which were the best so far. I was lucky enough to be in one of the newer ones on site, modern and very clean.

Work was to be in one of the concentrator buildings which is where the minerals are separated from the ore bodies, which contained mainly copper but also silver, lead and zinc. The copper was then sent to a smelting plant at Townsville on the coast by train about 900 kilometres east for further refining. The copper was pre-smelted on site into ingots of blister copper for transportation.

My introduction to my future workmates was quite funny if not frustrating. After completing my four hour induction on the first day at the mine and then going to the concentrator's work shop it was time to set to work. The guy taking me had called me Bill, my first name being William so he was quite correct calling me Bill but having always used my middle name Robert I corrected him twice to tell him I used Bob for my name. When we got to the workshop he took me to see the foreman and introduced me as Bill and then left. I told the foreman what name I used and that I was Bob not Bill .We talked a bit about this and that and then he took me into the workshop. It was lunchtime with a number of people there when he did a mass introduction of me to every one as the new electrician BILL! I thought *Stuff it, I'm Bill here.* And so the only time I was ever known by that name was at Mount Isa Mines.

It was nearly Easter before I moved on from Mount Isa and for most of that time my leisure activity was spent in the Irish Club which was in its very early stage of development - basically a large shed with picture windows and a bar along one wall. I revisited it in 2007 when our youngest daughter was living in Mount Isa, and it is now one of the largest social clubs in Australia.

Christmas of 1967 was a bit eventful, after I tripped rather badly on Christmas Eve and heard a sound like a snapping twig of wood and a sharp pain above my ankle. Being Christmas Eve and out on the town with a couple of Kiwi mates and an Irish mate I sort of ignored it. That was until the next day when I woke up with a swollen and painful leg just above my ankle. It was obvious that I needed to get it seen to so managing to hobble to the hospital I was berated by the doctor for not having been for some attention before then. A small bone had snapped in my leg and I was to spend the next five weeks in a half leg plaster cast. I was unable to work so I did not return to that until the end of January in the New Year. The Irishman and I had at this time rented a flat to share near the centre of town so I was close to shops and pubs and could keep myself busy chatting around town until the cast came off.

1968

Early in the New Year Mount Isa had some heavy rains, from storms raging all over North Queensland. Towards the end of January I returned to work and during that period the river that flows through the city centre was filled from what was a small trickle of water into a fast flowing river which now had raised the level to completely full. Fish were now visible in the water, and where they had come from is mind boggling. There were plenty of them and fairly big ones too. I can only surmise they were in the underground water system and got flushed out with the volume of water from the storms.

The roads in and out of the city from both east and west were flooded over in many places and impassable for traffic. The railway from the east was impassable due to flood damage also. The only mode of transport in or out was by air and even that was limited by the state of the weather. The road trains, which are two large trailers attached to a prime mover rig, were unable to make any deliveries of food or drink and this went on for almost two weeks before the food situation hit a point where there was not any fresh food to be bought. There was only a relatively small supermarket besides a couple of small outlets for fresh food items. It was at this point that the supermarket chartered a jet plane for grocery items and fresh food to be flown in from Adelaide. That eased the food problem but the beer situation was different. This is a beer-loving place and with only cans and bottles available, the next delivery of draught beer was eagerly awaited.

Saturday afternoon after knocking off from work at the mine had become a regular time for a few beers at one of the pubs in town. (I still have trouble referring to Mount Isa as a city due to its size. Crazy, hey, when it is probably the largest city in the world in land size). Anyway, on this particular Saturday I was waiting at the mine gate for the guy I used to go over to a pub with, to pick me up there. While I was waiting I spied a road train heading our way some distance away. When the guy I was waiting for pulled up for me I showed him the truck and we decided to wait to see what might be on it. Would you believe this piece of Australian logic? The truck was just loaded with beer kegs, the first and second trailers behind the prime mover were full of them and the rear trailer had beer kegs and also a few other boxes with them. Mount Isa sure had its priorities set in concrete! We followed the truck to its first drop off and this was our first port of call. When the beer had time to chill, things got back to normal from then on.

During January there were posters put around town telling of an upcoming Robbie Burns supper night at the RSL Club. There was a strong contingent of Scottish people in Mount Isa as well as many other countries. The fact that I had never been to one of these functions saw me purchasing a ticket to attend it. The night turned out to be very enjoyable with a bagpiper in attendance, who by the way, could be heard on many a balmy evening practising in the hills close to town. The feature of the supper was the Ode to the Haggis which anyone who was game got to taste. I was pleasantly surprised at the taste and even though that is the only time I have tasted one I still can remember it. Whisky of course was flowing in abundance.

Another recollection involving the Scots was at the Irish Club one Sunday afternoon when a Scottish student came in and became a part of the group that I was having a few beers with. He was a doctor's son from Edinburgh, travelling around Australia on a working holiday. He was interested in staying around for a while so we told him there would probably be work for him at the mine if he was to try for a job. The next day after work he found my Irish mate and me, and said he had a start for next day with first the four hour induction and then the foundry which was where the blister copper ingots were made. The foundry was the dirtiest place to work in on the surface where the smelting of the copper was done amongst other tasks. He was to be an assistant to the overhead crane crew. The surface workers' induction was the four hour session with a written test to conclude it. I had done the test when I started as a surface worker and got an average pass mark of around 75%. The student, who was on a break from university, told us after work that day that he had got a 100% pass and the company were so impressed he was sent into the drawing office to work instead of the foundry. He did only stay in Mount Isa for a few short weeks before moving on. I guess Australia was billed as the land of opportunity in the 60s so that little incident just went to show that it really was.

One activity I have never had any interest in is shooting. On one weekend my flat mate and a couple of Aussie mates were to go duck shooting at a dam some way from the mine and town. I was not very keen when they asked me if I wanted to go along. I told them I would not know one end of a rifle from the other but I was encouraged to give it a go, as the Aussies say. *Why not?* I thought.

The rifle I was loaned for the trip was a .22 rifle. It was after about a two hour drive on a gravel road that we arrived at the dam. There was just a small number of ducks on the water quite a distance away so we set ourselves down lying flat to the ground on the mound of the dam and lined them up. We were unable to shoot any ducks and even if we had I do not know how we could have retrieved them other than by a pretty long swim by someone. This next statement might sound a bit far-fetched but to this day I reckon my shots from the .22 were hitting the ducks but had lost any impact by the time the ducks were hit. The ducks would just hop off the water and then settle down again and that is the truth.

The other guys were quite amazed at the accuracy of my shooting for a novice!

It was coming on towards Easter and my two year period in Australia had passed by now; therefore, I figured it was time to leave Mount Isa and start heading back to Sydney, ready for returning to England. My bus ticket to Brisbane was still active so I got myself booked on to a bus to Townsville from where I would then change buses for Brisbane. Boarding the bus a few days later it was about 900 kilometres to Townsville, so an all-day bus ride at least was ahead of me and that was just to Townsville. The road was largely unsealed at this time and only about a half dozen or so small towns to pass through along the way. It was corrugated for long stretches through the vagaries of the weather, and this meant a pretty uncomfortable ride, but at least the bus had air conditioning and a toilet on board which helped to make it bearable. Arriving at Townsville I had a couple of days' stopover to have a look around and rest after the rattling bus ride. The only sealed sections of road were where they passed through the small towns, but it did get better as we came closer to Townsville, probably after we got to Charters Towers about 100 kilometres from there. Anyway after a couple of days there I continued on to Brisbane which was a much more comfortable ride on a sealed road.

Brisbane, QLD

After arriving at Brisbane I had a change of plan. Having re-membered that my mate from the road trip up to Queensland had left from here last year to go to New Zealand, that sent my thoughts the way they went. I figured it would be a good idea to make the effort and go to New Zealand myself while I was in this part of the world before making the trip back to England. There-fore, I booked an air ticket to make the trip across the Tasman

Sea. I arrived at Auckland, luckily with my survival kit of tools as I now had the intention of a short working holiday here.

Auckland, NEW ZEALAND

Arriving at Auckland the first thing I did after finding somewhere to stay was to check out what was required of me to do my job in New Zealand. It turned out that there was an office down in Wellington, the capital, for the business of Electrical Licensing. That meant I had to either do it by phone and mail, or go to Wellington and do the business there. After a couple of days looking around the city of Auckland that is just what I did. I went there on the train and a more scenic train ride I had never seen. The lake and mountain regions and the thermal steam eruptions around the areas which the train passed through were worth the effort I had made to come here. These steam eruptions provide the energy for the electricity production from the thermal power station there in the centre of the North Island of the country; this was the first in the world to do this. On a future visit to New Zealand I was to discover that the thermal activity there was part of the planet's safety valves for the thermal activity occurring below ground. These areas protect the planet from blowing itself apart, or so I was led to believe. I guess there is a certain amount of truth in that. After a really interesting journey the train finally passed through a valley region further south which led me into the city of Wellington.

Wellington, NZ

At Wellington I followed the routine of finding a couple of nights' accommodation so that I could check out the city and take things from there. The electrical licensing was the same as it had been in NSW and I was able to work on jobs which had another licensed electrician working there. I was in no hurry to apply for a licence myself in this situation as I had no desire to start sitting examinations at this time. I found a job in the city just by wandering onto the site of a large hotel which was being renovated; it was with the company that I was to spend about two months working for in and around the city.

Wellington turned out to be a quiet sort of city but a very scenic one. I spent most of my nights having a quiet walk around the city sampling a few beers or drinking coffee in some nice coffee shops. My weekends where a bit more adventurous, going to parks and having bus rides to places out of the city. The cable car to the top of Mt Victoria which dominates the skyline was well worth the trip, with terrific views across the city and the harbour. The Botanical Gardens were another nice place to spend a lazy weekend afternoon.

Friday afternoon here was the same as what happened in Aussie, with a few beers after work. There was a problem with that as the guys, most of whom were married family men, were still in the habit of leaving to go home at 6 pm, a throwback of the time of 6 o'clock closing days, I figured out. Ten pm closing had only been introduced around six months earlier so I guess that was the reason some of them would go to the bar to buy two jugs of beer at about 10 to 6 and knock them back quick as a flash before leaving. I had trouble understanding the reasoning behind that!

On one of my very first days in Wellington I experienced a day which proved why the city is commonly known as windy Wellington. A wind was giving the city a good work out when news filtered through that the ferry Wahine, which connects the two islands of North and South was in trouble on its crossing. The outcome was the sinking of the ferry which was a very sad time

51

here. She was a 9000 ton roll-on roll-off vessel, the biggest of its kind at the time, and fifty-one people died, not far off the coast at Wellington.

I considered going for a look at the South Island after I had been working here for about two months. However, I decided that it was about time I started to make a move back to Sydney and then onward on a return to England and home. With that in mind I went back to Auckland on the train after having booked a passage on a P&O liner leaving for Sydney from there.

Auckland

The train got me to Auckland the day before the ship was to sail. After one night in a hotel I boarded the ship next day to begin sailing for four days to Sydney across the Tasman Sea. This was my first experience of life on the ocean wave, and what an experience it then turned out to be! The cruise was on a P&O liner and it started in fine style with me being put into a four berth cabin which was obviously devoid of any other passengers. No other people had entered it by the time we set sail, and I therefore had the cabin to myself, which I was pretty happy about. I had chosen the first sitting for meals so at the time for dinner I went to the dining room and was directed to a small table for two people at which a young lady was already seated. She turned out to be a passenger on her way home to Cape Town in South Africa. We had a good conversation during the meal and as it was the first night at sea after a day in Auckland there were no activities that night other than Bingo. We arranged to catch up there for a drink.

Then things went pear-shaped because after a shower I lay on my bunk and got off it on a number of occasions, but mainly to go to the toilet block. The problem was the Tasman Sea. The ship

52

started to pitch and toss and the combination of dinner and pre-dinner drinks did nothing to help. The result was that I became very seasick. I actually lost track of time and a steward knocked on my door to see what was happening as he had noticed I was not getting about. He saw that I was in a state of sickness so he brought some bread rolls and a drink for me but the sea sickness would not stop. I just slept and spewed my way across the Tasman Sea. Once or twice I did go up to the upper decks but the ship was heaving so much and the wind and rain so heavy that I soon about-turned to the relative safety of my cabin. The steward tried to convince me that some fresh air would help but I was in no fit state to follow his advice. Then came the time when I eased myself off the bunk and realised that the ship had stopped rolling about and we must have sailed out of the storms. I showered and dressed myself and ventured to the upper decks to find the ship was tied up to Darling Harbour in Sydney!! The whole cruise had been spent sick as a dog below decks. That aside from the one meal I had on the first night.

My word, my first time at sea will never be forgotten. I some-times wonder if the young South African dinner companion reported my having gone missing and had anything to do with the steward taking an interest in my welfare. I then disembarked and found my mates across the bridge and re-joined them ready for the next step regarding my heading for England and home.

Sydney, NSW

My mate from Shaw was in Sydney and we were having drinks soon after this when I told him I was going to return home to be back with my family there. He said if that was so then he would go back as well, as he was ready to return too. We got ourselves to a travel agent and discussed what means were available for returning and decided a ship via the Pacific Ocean and Panama Canal would be a bit of fun as well as a means. I did have some reservations about having to cross the Tasman Sea again but took the chance that I would not have to put up with such wild weather two times running. I would also take the cabin steward's advice and make sure I ate some bread with my meals, certainly for the first few days of sailing. We booked passages with an Italian cruise company with a September sailing date.

As there were a couple of months before the ship sailed I told my mate that I would look for a job in the country to do some saving ready for the trip. There was an advertisement in the Sydney Morning Herald newspaper for electricians to work in the Snowy Mountains in NSW on the Hydro Electric Scheme. This was a project which by now must be nearly finished as far as the construction was concerned. I went for an interview and the work was to join the maintenance crew for the ongoing work involved with the project at Jindabyne. I was hired and booked on a flight to Cooma, and was to go to the local office there for directions to the site upon arrival.

Jindabyne, NSW

From Sydney the flight took me to Cooma and I made my way to the office in town. I was then taken to the town of Jindabyne and the site there. The town itself was very small, set alongside a lake and a real nice looking place to be for a while. My accommodation was in a camp near the township, a single cabin with meals provided in a canteen. I thought that Thredbo, the skiing resort nearby, could be handy for a weekend or two, but that was not to be. Unfortunately this turned out to be only a three or four day stay, as I was transferred to a small town called Talbingo. This change of course meant that my time here in Australia was more or less making a full circle with Talbingo just a very short distance from Adelong, the first real country job that I worked at.

My transport was by light aircraft and even that was worth coming here for, a very enjoyable flight across a large part of the Snowy Mountains area. The aircraft was a company one and was used for transporting people such as me around the project sites as well as making some deliveries of materials and mail etc. The flight reminded me of the time flying around the same area while in Adelong a couple of years previously but this time, no air sickness.

Talbingo, NSW

From the air there were snow-capped mountains below which made for a very enjoyable flight. We finally touched down at Talbingo which was being rebuilt because the old town would be flooded over by one of the lakes being part of the Snowy Mountain Scheme project. My job was mainly helping with joining back together houses which had been re-located to Talbingo from other project sites. It was also expected of me to be on call on a roster for the weekends to attend to any call outs on the site. There were single cabins which I was living in along with probably 20 or so other guys doing the same. Some of the houses were tenanted and a tavern had been built, that being the social hub along with a wet canteen on site. I do not recall a shop but with everything provided for me I was in no need of one other than for soap and toothpaste. Tumut, not far away, was a fairly large town so any things at all needed could be bought there.

There was a dam site close by which was under construction still, the third stage of construction with two other dams completed. I didn't ever work at the dam site, with all my work being done within the new township. Social life was limited on site to the tavern or the wet canteen at the quarters. It was on one of my weekends that I struck a bit of a mystery.

On the Sunday afternoon at around 4 pm someone came to my cabin to ask me to go to the tavern where it was opening time and the manager had no lights working there. I tried the lights with no response so going to the main switchboard I found someone had put a matchbox in between the faces of the magnetic coil which when energised should close together and so close the contacts to switch on the lights. Of course, removal of the matchbox fixed the problem. I put it down to someone playing a practical joke but that may or may not have been the case. That weekend was not my roster one and I had done a swap with one of the other guys who had wanted to go fishing. It seemed that the no lights at the tavern was not for the first time on Sundays, according to the manager, with no explanations for the faults. That was until yours truly came riding in on his white charger and came up with an answer. I was never to know if someone was playing practical jokes or not. I guess I will never know the reasons for those other faults! Shortly after that I returned to Sydney and caught up with my mate for the trip back to England.

Sydney, NSW

It was just a few days before we set sail for London. The time was spent with our mates there and I had a little tidy up job to do which was to become a bit embarrassing. I had taken out private health insurance before coming to Australia with a provider which had an office in Sydney. I decided to find it to cancel the cover as I was leaving the country. My payments had been made by mail every three months so consequently with all the travelling around that I had done in the two and a half years they had been accompanied with a change of address whenever I had moved on to a new one. I found the office which was fairly small, the provider being one of the lesser known companies. Anyway, I fronted up at the counter and when the lady attending it found out it was me she called the rest of the staff there to come and meet the man who they had been tracking for all that time. I guess I was there a fair while. Though not quite a coffee and cake morning, I gave a lot of explanations regarding the places I had been working around. The receptionist was nice to take an interest in all of that anyway.

Sydney to London

The day of the ship's departure came, so we were finally on board and getting sorted out in the cabin with two other passengers. One was a non-drinker as we found out and very quiet while the other was a big Italian guy who became one of the group of us who very soon became buddies, especially after the day's entertainment came to a close. We would congregate at a bar at the stern of the ship which was kept open for the late nighters; on occasions it was all-nighters. On these nights our Italian mate would get himself to the galley and his Italian mates there would load him up with fresh crusty bread rolls and hunks of cheese or salami for our snacks before getting off to our cabins for some sleep. It would be true to say that we slept for most of the days across the Tasman and woke in the late afternoon. We would then shower and have dinner before enjoying whatever the night's entertainment happened to be. Then it was to the back bar's night of merry making there. The sailing across the Tasman Sea was much kinder to me on this trip with no trouble at all with sea sickness.

Auckland, NZ

Our first stop was Auckland on a quiet Sunday morning, and we just had a walk around there. I guess once again, however, it would be true to say that all the late-nighters I had been participating in on board the ship had a fair bit to do with my lack of energy on this occasion.

Tahiti, SOUTH EAST PACIFIC

The next stopping place was Tahiti and that was much better. There was a nice surprise awaiting with the first sight of the islands. The view I got sailing towards them looked as if they had speared their way through the ocean's surface. It was a sight never to forget. There was an abundance of bright green vegetation covering the slopes of steeply inclined hills reaching for the sky, with deep blue sea complementing the scene. It was picture perfect.

We visited a beach at Papeete while we were there and for the evening's entertainment a resort had a floor show organised for the visiting passengers. All considered it was a very enjoyable few hours there. In later years I made trips to other Pacific islands but none of them have had the same impact on my first viewing of them as Tahiti did. From there the ship headed across the ocean eastwards towards Acapulco and the Panama Canal.

Acapulco, MEXICO

The ship anchored off shore here and a shuttle service of small tender boats ferried passengers to and from the town. Fronting the sea, the town was all glitz and glamour with a row of flash hotels and apartment blocks all along the sea front, but a walk two streets back was the complete opposite, not the part of Acapulco that appears on the tourism brochures here. There were street sellers all over the place back around the glitzy bit, who were not too pleased with people not wanting to buy. I did buy a Mexican sombrero and the last I saw of that it was decorating a wall in my home in Oldham after giving it to my parents as a gift. Here was a place where a shore excursion might have been a better option than visiting the town, it being a bit of an anti-climax. We were back on board the ship early here.

Panama, CENTRAL AMERICA

The Panama Canal crosses the Isthmus of Panama and was, back then, the most direct route to take by ship. Gatun Lake is a lake (33 kilometres long) which is part of the canal, but it is 26 metres above sea level, so there are three locks at each end. At the time it was built, Gatun Lake was the largest man-made lake in the world, and the dam was the largest dam on Earth.

When our ship entered the Panama Canal I spent some time watching the operations ashore for the first set of three locks. We would later cross the lake to be lowered down by a system of three more locks to the Caribbean Sea side of the canal and then into the Atlantic Ocean. It was an early night to bed that night in readiness for the shore visit next day. Upon waking, I went out on deck to see that we were sailing across the lake. The water was very still and there was an eerie feeling in the early morning light. The humidity was oppressing with hardly a breath of air to cool the watching passengers down. After having breakfast it was time for the few hours on shore at Cristobal.

We had been warned on the ship to be very careful where we went while ashore due to the political unrest of the area. We were told that the city was patrolled in two halves which were separated by an imaginary line running down the centre of the main road. One half was patrolled by servicemen from the USA and the other by local servicemen. We were warned to only go into the area controlled by the USA. A group of four of us went ashore and the division of the two sectors was soon be seen. The USA men were out in force, obvious I guess because of the passengers being about in large numbers. They kept a strict eye on us making sure we would not get ourselves into the danger of crossing to the other side. In fact, there were just as many local servicemen patrolling the other side as there were on our side, I reckon. The batons swinging by their sides would be enough to put anyone off from going over there. It soon became obvious that this was not going to be a very enjoyable visit to the city so the four of us made our way back to the ship for a cool beer or two for the rest of the time there. We were not alone, I might add. Later that day the ship set sail for Willemstad in the Dutch West Indies in the Caribbean Sea which was to be our next port of call and much more enjoyable. Panama had been quite an experience.

Willemstad, CURACAO

Arriving at Willemstad, the capital city of Curacao, after leaving Panama it looked more welcoming and peaceful here. The buildings were very brightly decorated with many colours evident. I went on shore with the same three mates as before and we set about looking around the city centre of Willemstad which has a huge oil refinery nearby. We had a beer or two and then asked someone how far it was to a beach. We were told it was about a half hour walk from where we were so we set off. It was the middle of the day and pretty hot and humid, not really walking weather. As we walked down the road I spied a bar just up a driveway on our right. I said to the others, how about a pit stop for a beer and some cool shade for a while. We all agreed that was a good idea so up to the building and into the bar we went. There was a good selection of bottles behind the bar on the shelves so it looked as if a long stay might be on the cards so to speak. We sat ourselves at a table by the window and a man with his white shirt and black trousers asked if he could help us. I asked him what kind of beer there was and he said there was Tiger beer. I ordered four of them and he went behind the bar and brought out the four bottles of beer. With that I said to him how much are they and we were all very apologetic when he said, "Oh no sir, no charge. This is my house and you are my guests."

Talk about embarrassing! He was real nice about it however, and it has to go down as another moment to remember.

We did find the beach and there was a resort hotel with quite a few of the other passengers from the ship there as well. It turned out to be a good afternoon and our return to the ship went to the back of the mind. That meant a last minute dash in taxis for quite a few of us. I was all for staying on at the island when we got back to the ship but the Master at Arms made sure that we all got on board again. He ordered me to our cabin or it would be a night in the brig. Taking his advice was the finish of a very good day out. From there it was a sail across the Atlantic Ocean to Lisbon in Portugal.

Lisbon, PORTUGAL

The ship was just out of Lisbon by a couple of days when there were two incidents for mentioning. The first was a trap shooting competition on board. There were a number of entrants and they slowly reduced as people missed the clay pigeons when released

61

off the stern of the ship. There would be two of the clay pigeons catapulted upwards and the entrants had two shots which had to hit them. It got down to the final two, one of whom was our Italian cabin mate. He was up against another guy and they went neck and neck until our mate missed one which meant the other guy was the winner. The problem was it was our mate's first shot and so in his frustration he shot a seagull clean out of the sky with his second shot. What a commotion that caused, with booing and catcalls especially from the females watching. It was not a pretty sight, with just white feathers floating on the surface of the sea. He made a hasty retreat, with all that was going on about it.

The other incident would have been the following day when I was in one of the lounges enjoying a game of cards with some other passengers. The day was very foggy and all of a sudden the ship lurched quite quickly over to the left. The cards and other paraphernalia went scattering to the floor and the ship then leaned over the other way righting itself. I managed to look through one of the windows as this was happening and even though it was foggy I could see the hulk of another ship pretty close to ours. That must have been one heck of a near miss out there. I think we all counted our blessings that day.

We arrived at Lisbon in the late evening and the ship was to leave for London very early next morning. That meant we just enjoyed a night out on the town, with no repeat of the Willemstad departure thank goodness. Our little group were back on board in good time for some sleep before the ship left port.

London, ENGLAND

The ship docked in the late afternoon and there at the dockside were my parents to meet us. They were accompanied by a family friend who shared a house with my aunt and uncle's family in Harrow where I had spent many a holiday period when I was a schoolboy. We drove back to Harrow where we spent the night with them. Next day the four of us went up north to Oldham on a coach which is where my mate and I parted company to resume living at our old homes. We did of course get to spend lots of time over beers during the time we were back home. On the coach ride the view through the windows struck me as being so different from what I had seen in Australia. The thing that struck me the most was the difference in the air cleanliness. The whole of the countryside here had a thin bluish haze about it, no doubt from the exhausts of traffic and industry. I realised then just how clean and fresh it had been for the last two and a half years.

Oldham

It took a few days to get around all of my old friends and family when we got back to the town, and following that it was time to think about a job. The firm I had worked for before leaving had closed up shop and was no longer in business. A friend of the family told me a firm in town was always looking out for workers, not electrical but working at a steel warehouse. I had never done anything other than electrical work so I thought, *Why not for a change?* So I went over to the place and was given a start. It only took two days for me to get hopelessly bored with that. I had been warned that the job had a high turnover of workers and I was no exception. Just sheet after sheet of sheet metal to sort into piles of same thicknesses from job lots. The boss was OK about such a short stay so I looked for something I knew would keep me interested.

That was a job with a large electrical firm in Oldham and I was delegated to go to a woollen mill just out of town with an apprentice to do the work of converting the lighting to a more modern system than what was there. It was towards the end of September by now and I did stay on there until the wanderlust got into me again just after Christmas when I started looking into doing something else overseas.

1969

The first idea I had was to investigate the opportunity of going to Canada to live for a while. There was a Canada House in Manchester for processing applications for this so I went there for interviews. The end product of all that was a job on the Churchill Dam project which was to supply hydro power for Labrador and Newfoundland. When I was at the interview I was all for going but later the thoughts in my head were remembering the good times I had in Australia and how it was now summer over there and winter in Canada. I was up front with the Canadian guy who had been attending to me and he said that my decision was up to me of course. That was when I decided to have another trip back to sunny Australia.

Southampton, ENGLAND

It had been a real good time with my family and friends for the four months or so, and after this I booked myself on a passage on a ship from Southampton to Fremantle in Western Australia via South Africa. When departure time came along I was sent on my way with good wishes from everyone.

I was allocated a berth in a four-berth cabin, sharing with three other young blokes and the four of us soon got acquainted over a beer or two. This turned out to be a really good trip which kicked off after the first port of call at the Canary Islands. By then I guess you could say we had become good buddies.

CANARY ISLANDS

The four of us went ashore as a group and really just spent the time exploring the port town of Las Palmas and having a drink or two there. To be truthful I was a bit disappointed with the state of the town where we went ashore, nothing like what I had expected. I had visions of a tropical paradise which it may well be away from the town but here was a place which seemed not very nice at all, perhaps once again a shore excursion may have been a better option. The stopover was only for a few hours which was not enough time to give the island a fair chance to impress.

After the time ashore we sailed in the afternoon so we then settled down to having a chat in the main lounge. We were joined by an older guy who had spent a bit of time previously in our company. We were just chatting about this and that when one of the crew came to join us at our table. He was the purser and along with his clipboard he was out raising volunteers to join in a talent show that was to be one of the activities on board in a couple of days' time during the afternoon. I myself did not need much encouraging to sing if I had been having a few beers and that was my contribution to the discussion basically, one of the other guys said he had his guitar with him and had been in bands before. The older guy was a retired bandmaster from his days in the Army, so what chance did we have of not performing? The other two guys were happy to join in so the purser asked us for a name for our group and seeing as we had been complaining between ourselves about the cabin being a bit smelly from our socks we became 'The Sweaty Feet Four'. The bandmaster guy offered to help us arrange some songs if we would like him to.

We had two days to rehearse two songs which we did in a cabin sort of office for a couple of hours each day. The afternoon of the show came and our performance was well received by the audience so we were pretty happy about that. Our song, 'Johnny is a Joker' went down extra well thanks to the bandmaster guy giving his tips on presentation. There had been about eight other acts and probably 15 or so people got up to do their thing.

After the show had finished the five of us sat down for a few drinks together when who should come along but the purser. He had his clipboard again and told us that seeing as we were game enough to do the talent show he hoped we would be part of the shows that would be put on during the course of the voyage. Of course we agreed to that having broken the ice with what we had just done. The same applied to everyone who had been up on the stage that afternoon so the trip really kicked on from then onwards.

We were told that there would be three shows performed on the trip before reaching Sydney so that meant quite a number of rehearsals. I pointed out to the purser that I was only travelling as far as Fremantle but he was not put out by that and said that would be no problem. The first show was to be an Hawaiian night and rehearsals for that were the first ones with the show scheduled for before the next port of Cape Town. The rehearsals were held on the entertainment nights which finished up reasonably early in the main entertainment lounge, nights such as trivia or bingo nights. The lounge would then be shut for rehearsals, which took about two hours and the good thing was that the bar opened up for about another hour, with plenty of free drinks. The three shows were to be firstly the Hawaiian night followed by a Roaring 20s night and finally a Wild Western night. That one I missed as it was after Fremantle. All the passengers were invited to dress for the themes and the costumes for ourselves performing were all on hand for us to use. There were two songs for 'The Sweaty Feet Four' to learn for each show. With all of that it turned out to be quite a busy time for us but really enjoyable. I think our bandmaster mate was enjoying the time just as much as we were. Time seemed to fly and the first show came and went without a hitch, with many a laugh along the way.

Cape Town, SOUTH AFRICA

The ship sailed into the bay where Cape Town lies, on a fine day, and a clear view of Table Mountain greeted us. We docked after breakfast, and had until late afternoon for time ashore. I headed up the road towards the mountain with one of my cabin buddies. It was good to stretch our legs but we decided it was going to be too far, so did an about turn and headed back towards the city centre. As it was around lunchtime we went into a pub for a bite to eat along with a couple of beers. The pub was a pretty small one, just a bar room really and we were into our second beer when a coloured man came in through the door. He had not taken more than one step into the room before the barman ordered him out with the words that this was a white man bar. He immediately turned around and left without a word. Of course, apartheid was the law of South Africa at this time and I guess that was not an unusual happening. There were two or three other guys in the bar and one of them left soon afterwards. It would have been no more than two minutes before he came back in bleeding quite badly having been accosted by coloured men outside. My mate and I then got more than a bit nervous about leaving ourselves, after that episode. The barman told us that we would have to leave the main road to get attacked and said so long as we kept on the main road we should be OK. As it turned out we got back to the city without any trouble but not the best of days out, I was not sorry to get back on board after that. Shades of the day I had been ashore at Panama on the trip back to England.

When the ship left Cape Town things soon got back to normal on board. We got to do the Roaring 20s show and all went well with that. As the ship approached Fremantle, the port city close to Perth, it was time to bid farewell to my cabin buddies and the friends I had made from the shows. The purser gave me his best wishes which was nice of him, and so at the docks next day I left to resume life in Aussie again. The Ten Pound Pom had returned!!

Perth, WA

Using local transport I got into Perth and found myself over-night accommodation ready for seeking work the next day. The first thing I had to do was organise another permit from the electrical licensing board to work here in WA. Here I was told that I would have to sit an examination within six months or the permit would be cancelled. There would not be a third permit if I did not do that. Setting about finding a job was the next thing on my agenda. It was a change of tack this time, not with the newspaper advertisements but with a handful of five cent coins and a phone book in a call box. I found the electrical contractors in the phone book and set about making calls. It did not take long to get an interview and then a job. It was for a firm who did work at a bottling factory so that was the first few days of working. I found a guest house in the city for accommodation until I had sourced a job in a country area which I asked for at my interview. I had been told there was work of that nature with them.

That job came about within a few days when I was told some-one was needed on the work they did at Exmouth which is about 1300km north of Perth on the Exmouth peninsular up the coast. I was not sorry to leave the factory as in the bottling plant the noise of the empty bottles rattling against each other was pretty disturb-ing to say the least. I think annoying would be a better description of the noise. Anyway I flew up to Exmouth and was met at the airstrip by the company supervisor and driven into the township, then on to the camp where I was to be billeted along with guys from a building company also there doing work.

Exmouth, WA

The cabins at the camp here were made of corrugated iron, two of them each with twelve rooms, six either side of a centre corridor and an entrance door at either end. The whole building was tied to the ground with hoops made of tubular pipe circling up one side, across the roof and down the other side, the ends embedded in concrete down below the surface of the ground. In a few months' time we were to rely on the structure when Exmouth was in the direct line of a cyclone and our safety was on account of it being so secure. There was an ablution block and also a mess room for meals with two guys who were the best cooks I had on any camp anywhere. All in all I had a very good job here. The camp was situated on the corner of the United States naval base on the peninsular just a short drive out of the township of Exmouth, completely separated from the base with a high wire fence and a locked gate. There was high security surrounding access to the base and all of the guys at the camp had dog tags to allow them to go into it for work. Most of the jobs were for the navy so that was a daily occurrence for most of them.

The job for us was the installation of a refrigeration plant which was to be used to cool down the huge cables which were connected to the antennae for transmitting signals to the submarines out in the ocean. Antennae were strung in the air at heights of over 1000 feet and looped around thirteen towers in a star shaped pattern. There was a huge amount of static electricity in the air and I was led into the trap of getting up onto a delivery truck to help with the unloading of materials for the job. I found out that all new starters were given this task because unknown to me there

70

was a length of insulated cable lying on the ground with one end connected to a copper rod driven into the ground. This was used to touch any metal to be unloaded and short any static charge from any metal on board to ground. Without doing that a rather large electric shock was felt when you became the shorting element. Laughter all round from the guys on the ground of course. The static was so strong in the surrounding air that you could just hold a fluorescent light tube in your hands and it would be fully lit. The base was just for communication with the submarines and consequently there were no ships here.

We were a tight little group at the camp as time went on. There were two of us there from our firm with the supervisor living in a house in the township with his wife and young family. They were an English family from Birmingham and real nice. The builders who owned the camp had a dozen men there, all carpenters and brick layers. Then there were the two cooks who also did any of the other duties needed around the camp. The only other electrician there was to become a good friend for life and we are still good mates today. It turned out that I was to be his best man at his wedding in 1975.

We had a pretty good social life revolving around the pub, which is a resort these days. I recently googled Exmouth and there has been quite a change there with even the Naval Base now a resort hotel. There was a hall in the town, where we enjoyed many functions on Saturday nights, including dances. I stayed at Exmouth for about a year and a half with a short gap in the middle which will unfold as I go on, basically I was away from there for about six weeks.

Shortly after arriving at Exmouth I received paper work regarding the examination to obtain a full licence to work. My supervisor was the observer for the purpose of making sure I kept to the rules regarding time and resources such as text books etc. I passed the exam, and there was now a practical exam to be done at my earliest convenience. I would be assessed by a travelling inspector on his next visit to the Exmouth area.

There was one day when I believe I met the king of horse race tipsters at the Picnic Race meeting which was held during Gala week in Exmouth. A third electrician had joined us by this time and the three of us had been transferred from the camp to live at a small tourist resort, which was much better than the camp, with people coming and going all the time. A young married couple were there on a holiday at the time of the race day and they decided to join the three of us to go there. There were probably seven or eight races and by the time the fourth one came around the young bloke had backed all the winners so far. We asked him how he had managed to do that and his reply was he looked for a big horse with the glossiest sheen. He went on to pick every winner that day. It was a good night out at the lodge after that with a barbecue dinner serving Spanish mackerel caught during the game fishing activities which were also a feature of Gala week.

Soon after this I went to Perth for a short while as the work here had dropped off a bit. Two of us went, leaving just the one electrician and the supervisor. We would be returned to Exmouth after about six weeks when new contracts would be started. I had decided to take a two week break from work and fly to Sydney and catch up with my mates there. The two of us arrived at Perth airport and I found a direct connecting flight travelling on what is known as the Red Eye, a flight that leaves Perth about midnight for the trip to Sydney. I was lucky to have the only seat in a three seat space so was able to lie down across the seats and get some good sleep, blanket and pillow provided by the stewardess. In Sydney I got to stay with my mates at Neutral Bay in the house they were sharing. It was a good two weeks with them and we had a few good nights out and about. The trip back to Perth was again by air, and I had work at a new women's prison being built just outside of the city at Middle Swan. As the job was a fair way out of the city I splashed out and bought myself a small car, a Mini, which was very handy for the weekends to do some serious sightseeing around the city's outskirts.

While I was in Perth I figured it would be a good idea to try to get my electrician's licence sorted out. At the Technical College I was told that a practical examination was being held at the college in Fremantle the following week, so I enrolled on the spot, did the exam and got a favourable pass mark. Having already done the written test I was now fully licensed for work in Western Australia. I had rented a small flat just two streets back from the beach while in Perth midway between the city and Fremantle. This was handy while relaxing sometimes on a weekend and with the city not far away was good also for a bit of clubbing on the Saturday nights. At the end of November I was told that the work in Exmouth was ready to go again so I then drove the Mini up there.

The drive went well for most of the way. I had left Perth pretty early, at about 7 am, and planned on being up at the roadhouse at the Exmouth turnoff from the highway by evening. That was where I would leave the road which goes along the coast of WA, and go along the peninsula road for the 150 kilometre drive to Exmouth. I got to the roadhouse and was planning to stay there for the night but after having a meal I decided to carry on and get the ride over and done with. I had been on a sealed road all day but the road I was now on was unsealed and very dusty. Things were still going OK when darkness came, at least that was until the ignition light on the dashboard lit. I reckoned I was a bit over half way so I decided that if I drove without my lights on the battery might get me to Exmouth. It was a bright moon, so it was easy enough to see, and there was no other traffic on the road.

All was well and I kept going, that was until a big kangaroo was parked right in the middle of the road and I was unable to do anything other than stop. The kangaroo ambled off into the scrub as the engine died, and a restart was met with dead silence. It was then about 10 pm so I just sat and waited for someone to come along. That did not happen until about 5 am next morning when the postal delivery van came along. The driver packed me into the van and took me the six kilometres into Exmouth. I was only an hour's walk from there, and if only I had known that I could have walked into town but the wait was not too uncomfortable. The driver of the van kindly dropped me off at my supervisor's house, and he took me back to the Mini and gave me a tow to the local garage. A new generator fixed the problem. The garage mechanic suggested that the gravel road from Manilya had shaken the generator up to cause the problem.

There were only two towns passed through in the 1300 kilometres between Perth and Exmouth - Geraldton at the 430 kilometre mark and Carnarvon at the 920 kilometre mark with the Manilya Roadhouse a further 140 kilometres away from there. There was then the 150 kilometres to Exmouth on gravel road. Just throwing in a little trivia here to put those distances into perspective, a lap of driving around Australia from Perth and back to Perth for example would be a minimum of 20,000 kilometres, a huge country indeed. I arrived to find that our accommodation had been resumed at the camp by the base so it was a virtual restart here, after six weeks away.

One weekend two of the crew here suggested we drive to Coral Bay in the Mini to visit the new pub which had been built there. Coral Bay was being developed from a place with a few shacks to a big resort, about 100 kilometres south of Exmouth. It is now the centre for visits to the Ningaloo Reef offshore of Coral Bay. The two other guys on site were carpenters from New Zealand. I was to get into some serious trouble with one of them but more of that further on.

We left town that weekend on the Sunday planning a few beers at the new hotel while checking it out. We were rolling along quite well going south on the road to the turn off to Coral Bay. The gravel road had not given any problems to the Mini this time. Then we reached the turnoff and this road was little more than a track. That was OK until we got to a dry creek bed about 15 metres across with a slight depression in the middle. The bed was made up of small round rocks rather like large pebbles washed smooth by the years of flow when the creek was running.

The Mini got into the middle and then would not gain any traction to go up the slight incline to the other side. It would not get any traction to reverse out either so there we were stuck fast in the middle of the creek bed. We attempted to push the car in either direction and no go there either, just a bit too slippery for us so out came the thinking caps. Then one of the Kiwis spotted two sheets of corrugated roofing iron bent all shapes and so obviously used on many occasions by people finding themselves in the same predicament as we were now in. We had a chat about what might be best to do: use the iron to go forward and risk not getting back, or backwards and come again in a bigger car next time. That option was the answer, so by placing the sheets close up to the tyres we were able to get out of the situation and made our way back to the camp.

We made the trip there again soon after, this time on a Saturday with a tent and some sleeping gear. Two other guys from the camp came along as well, one of whom had a station wagon. We made it OK and had a terrific weekend there. The pub was real nice and right by the beach which is where I slept in the dunes after a good night at the pub. We continued partying next morning in the pub after congregating there for breakfast. We rolled up into the dining room and ordered something to eat which was when I spied a wine rack close to the wall just behind my seat. I asked the waitress if we could have a bottle then and she told us that alcohol could not be served with breakfast. However, when she had gone away with the order we decided it would be a good idea to get a bottle from the rack, pour it around the five of us into the coffee cups and hide the bottle under the table. This ruse worked for the duration of the meal and by the time the waitress had realised what we were up to we had consumed a couple of bottles. She was not amused but when we showed her the empty bottles and said to add the cost to the bill she relaxed her feelings on the matter and we just paid up and left with no more said about it.

Later on the beach, I made a similar mistake to the one I had made at Bondi beach the first week I was in Sydney. I fell asleep in the dunes again sometime after lunch and the outcome of that was a suntan a bit over the top. Sunburn is a more suitable description.

Christmas came along and the company had left word for our supervisor to treat the three of us there to Christmas drinks. This was not unusual as he would every week on a Friday afternoon tell us to be at the pub at 4pm where he would put a $20 note on the table and that would cover the cost of drinks until he left for his home in town. These afternoons did not end after the money was spent; they almost always turned into late nights with the locals at the pub. Christmas Day was spent with our supervisor and his family in the afternoon which was really enjoyable.

1970

About now one of my Kiwi mates and I got ourselves into the trouble previously mentioned. The Navy Base had a social club on their site which was used quite often for entertainment for the sailors. The nickname used for them was Sea Bees, I never did get to know why! They of course were often in the pub enjoying beers just like we were. The two of us were enjoying a Saturday night at the pub when one of the Sea Bees mentioned that a dance was on at their social club and that was where they were going next. We could not be included as a 24 hour pass was needed for any guests to attend their social club.

When the pub closed we took a couple bottles of beer back to our camp and were sitting on the outside steps of our rooms chatting. We could hear the sound of music drifting across from the base and made the stupid decision to check the gate at the rear of our camp into the base. The only security on this gate was a chain and padlock, the main entrance at the front of the base being permanently manned by security staff. The chain was loose enough to squeeze through the gap when the gate was pushed so we did just that. We got to the social club only to be asked for our passes which we did not have. The Sea Bee at the door then went inside to make enquiries and suddenly a large black car with Aussie and USA flags on the front wheel arches drew up alongside us. Two military policemen got out and one of them opened the rear door for a man with enough medals on himself to sink a ship. He had a brown uniform and was obviously the boss cocky of the base. He asked us what we were doing there and before I could say anything (and some politeness was certainly called for in this situation) my Kiwi mate gave him a bit of lip. That settled it.

We were bundled into the car and taken to a room in the building at the main gates. We were there for about 20 minutes when a

Sea Bee came into the room with a camera and a wooden T-bar with which he took mug shots of the two of us. Probably another hour later we were taken out of the room into another one and in there was the guy who the remark had been made to, the local Commonwealth policeman who I knew from my work around the town, my supervisor and the Kiwi's boss. We were asked to explain ourselves, and then put back into the other room for about another hour before being brought out again. Then the security Sea Bees told us to leave the base and go back to our camp and to not even look backwards, just go. My supervisor told me it had been sorted out and to see him on Monday at work.

The following morning I went into town in the company truck like I always did to get the Sunday newspapers for the guys at the camp. I ran into the Commonwealth copper there and he told me not to ever pull a stunt like last night's again. He said the phone lines to Canberra, England, New Zealand and USA had run hot and he reckoned the US Navy now would know the colour of my grandmother's eyes. My supervisor was not very amused at having to spend all his time in the early hours of Sunday morning doing what he did but said nothing more about it.

When February came along there were cyclone warnings being given out, and this was the time that the accommodation roof was put to the test. The warnings started on about a Tuesday and were increased in severity daily until on the Friday afternoon the final warning came to get into a safe place. The weather had turned to rain and strong winds. I was working at the town school on an extension being built there at the time so I packed things away and made my way to the camp. That turned out to be a bit of a mistake because only four or five of us living at the camp went there. The rest of the guys made their way to the pub, stupid me hey. Anyway, we were not to get away from the camp until the following Monday night. The wind increased in strength to reach a maximum of 214 kilometres per hour and it was quite terrifying to sit through that.

I had parked my Mini at the gable end of the rooms and I could just see the front bumper by looking down along the side of the building through my window. The front of the car was almost being lifted from the ground and was in a continual rocking motion when I took a look. There were missiles flying past which were really sheets of corrugated roofing iron from who knows where. One of them actually sliced through the roof and the corner of it pierced through the ceiling of the room of one of the other guys. The eye of the cyclone passed over us after what seemed like an eternity and all of us at camp decided that if we were quick about it we could race over to the canteen and grab some food to take to our rooms, as we had sat through many hours without any. The air was as still as could be at that point and the silence was deafening.

We had not been back in our rooms for very long before the whole thing started to blow again. Without a doubt, I would never want to experience another cyclone ever. When the weather had changed for the better the first thing I went to check was my Mini. Raising the bonnet I saw smooth sand with the underside of the bonnet impressed into the sand, an engine compartment completely filled with sand. The beach was about 500 metres away from the camp too. I hosed the sand out and thankfully there was no damage caused.

When I drove into town there were dead fish which had been blown out of the sea onto the roadway, and one house had its roof lying in the garden alongside the house. The town was a mess with upturned boats blown around, litter everywhere and the caravan park was a complete mess as well. We three electricians were kept busy for the next few days restoring power and repairing overhead power lines around the town. That was how the tropical cyclone which gave Exmouth a visit had her effect on me!

The clean-up from the cyclone had been done when one of the electricians decided to leave along with one of the carpenters to take a trip to Europe. We had become good mates by now and I told him that I was intending to make another trip to England myself in the not too distant future. He asked me for a contact phone number and would see about a catch up when they got to England themselves so I gave him my parents' phone number before they left. I left Exmouth a short time after that and drove my car back to Perth after having booked a passage back to Athens in Greece for starters for the first leg of my journey back to England.

Perth, WA

I booked on what were Ship/Jet Tours at the time from Fremantle to Athens, sold my car back to the dealer I had bought it from and joined the cruise liner for the first leg of the journey at Fremantle. The liner was a Russian one which was to sail across the Indian Ocean to Djibouti in what was then French Somaliland in the Horn of Africa on the north-eastern coast. From there a jet would fly me to Athens in Greece, hence the name Ship/Jet Tour. After arriving in Athens with a hotel booked for an overnight stay, I would be completing the journey to England under my own steam.

The sail across the Indian Ocean was pretty uneventful with just socialising on the ship but next to no entertainment on board. I guess one thing that springs to mind needing a mention is my first and only encounter with the Russian delicacy which is touted as a must-have food but I found it disgusting. Why some people rave on about this delicacy is way beyond my comprehension. I did give it a chance by eating most of the serving but no thanks for repeating that exercise. The delicacy was of course, caviar. The Russians can have it all to themselves.

Djibouti, DJIBOUTI

It was hot, dry and dusty on arrival here. My flight ticket was already organised for the same day as the ship docked so not a real lot of time for exploring around the town, just time enough to find the airline office for checking out the transport to the airport and then a walk around to check out anything of interest. Poverty was quite apparent with women queueing at a hand-driven communal pump for filling tin cans and plastic bottles with water. It was made quite obvious to me that I was not welcome to watch this activity so I put a bit of distance between us fairly quickly.

Another sight to behold was a butcher's stall in a market place. The meat was hanging on the outside of the stall in the hot sun and was inundated with flies. People were buying the meat so I guess there was no alternative really. It was drummed into me just how lucky we are in our culture with clean food and running water at our fingertips.

Athens, GREECE

The first thing to strike me at Athens was the hustle, bustle and noisy traffic in the city. Probably the reason for that was having spent over a year in the small country town of Exmouth. (The traffic over there was anything but noisy.) I decided early on to make the Parthenon site my first place to visit after a quiet night at my hotel. I easily soaked up the culture of the place when I got there and was deep in thoughts of how it must have been back in the olden days. The stone about the place was very weather-worn from years of exposure, and restoration was being done to many of the areas there. By the end of the day, having walked from the hotel up to the site and back, combined with all that walking around I was pretty leg weary. I spent the next day wandering around the city with a snack I can still taste in my mouth. It was the sweetest, most sickly thing I have ever tried to eat. The lady at the stall did try to put me off but it looked much more inviting than it really was.

As this was my first time in Europe I intended to travel by land and sea on my way to England. Planning Rome as my next stopover I looked at options to get there from Athens. There was a ferry boat from Patras on the west coast to Brindisi in Italy off the Adriatic Sea, then a train on to Rome, so that became my next move. So I got on a bus which took me to Patras with a bridge crossing of the narrow Corinth Canal on the way. I found the terminal for the ferry which I caught the next day to Brandisi, then caught the first available train to Rome. It was on the train that I got chatting with an English couple who lived at Ashton near Oldham. Ashton was the same town the bloke was from who freely gave the bore water at Sapphire in Queensland. Guess I should make the effort to visit Ashton someday, incredible that I have never made a visit there and only a few short miles to do so from home at Oldham. They were a married couple in their 40s I reckon and easy to get along with. They offered me their company while doing any sightseeing in Rome so I took them up on that. We all booked into a hotel in Rome for three or four days.

Rome, ITALY

At breakfast the next day an Aussie couple got to chatting with us and also became part of our sightseeing group. Although I am finding this a bit hard to believe, somehow or other a young American bloke also staying there joined our group. We did walking tours of the city to such places as the Colosseum, St Peter's Square and numerous other Roman landmarks. We would also make a note of interesting-looking restaurants for our evening meal on that particular day. One of the highlights was a train ride to Pompeii and a walk around the ruins there, which are from the volcanic eruption of Mt Vesuvius in 79 AD. There are actual bodies encased in the lava which inundated the site. The thing that surprised me a lot was the distance of the mountain from the 'burial' site. It must have been a very powerful eruption to send the erupting lava and debris such a long distance and still catch the people so unawares of the oncoming tragedy. One of the bodies is actually in a cowering posture and must have been totally unable to get away from the devastation of the eruption.

One of our evening meals was particularly memorable because it happened to be the restaurateur's birthday that day and he really turned on a night to savour with a constant supply of wine and much merrymaking. It had been three really good days in Rome and now I looked forward to my next stopover, Paris. The train was my transport from Rome via Florence and Milan, so I had short visits to these two cities between connections. From Milan I had a sleeping berth to Paris. I was surprised to see the station at Lucerne in Switzerland blanketed in snow, as it was towards the end of May, and it was nice to watch the snow-covered country-side roll by for a while. Arriving at Paris I found a hotel close to the railway station, and stayed for three nights.

Paris, FRANCE

Paris was pretty much a repeat of Rome with more walks around the city taking in the landmarks. One afternoon and evening was spent at Montmartre with its bars taking up much of my time there. I have to admit that I struggled to find my way back to the hotel after that one and had to resort to a taxi. That proved embarrassing when I discovered that I had not enough money to cover the fare. I gave the driver what I had and I know he was not happy about that. It was his own fault really because when I had hailed him for the ride I had asked him to take me as close as he could to the hotel for the amount of money that I had in my pockets, which was 70 francs. When he pulled up at the hotel I was real happy that was where it had got me. Unfortunately, it turned out that 70 francs was not enough for the fare he had on his meter. He was not at all happy about the misunderstanding but there was nothing that I could do about it until I could get to a bank the next day so I made a hasty retreat into the hotel. No *gendarmes* came around so I guess he left it at that with a few choice French words to follow me. From Paris I had a train ride to Calais to catch a ferry across the English Channel.

Calais

There was a Channel ferry at Calais when I arrived there so I went on that to Dover. It was the first time for me seeing the White Cliffs and I can still remember the joy I felt at seeing my home country again. London was my next stop with a visit to the bank to get some money from the deposit I had set up there. Before leaving Australia I had made a point of having enough money in England to fund a couple of months' holiday at my parents' house and a fare back to Aussie in case I wanted to return again. This was also done for the two future visits I was to make before 1977 came around.

I caught a train to Manchester and then the local bus to Shaw a couple of miles out of Oldham to where my parents had moved to live while I had been in Exmouth. I had phoned them from London and a hot dinner was waiting for me when I arrived there.

Shaw, ENGLAND

I had mixed feelings arriving in Shaw, because I was not sure what would be next. Should I find a job or just take things easy and go back to Australia after a few weeks there? My answer came quite quickly as one of my old mates from before I left for the first time came to see me. When the business we worked for then closed down he and another of the electricians had used their payout to open their own electrical contracting business and asked if I might be interested in working for them. It was the ideal solution really, as they accepted that I may not be a long time proposition which suited them also. So began my re-uniting with them, with lots of stories about our times working together back then. It proved a bit harder to get back into the swing of things socially, as most of my old friends had now been married for some time and had young families. There was only my mate from Aussie still around as a single bloke. There was of course time spent with the others and we are still to this day good friends. The job with my old workmates was most suitable for me, re-lighting a section of an old cotton mill not so far from Shaw.

September came, and my mate from Exmouth contacted me when he arrived in London. He was with his travelling mate so my parents told me to invite them to stay with us at the house. They came a few days afterwards and I drove them around visiting Blackpool and the Lake District and places in between. It was my impression that the two mates were very surprised to find England was so open with lots of countryside to pass through. It is not uncommon for Aussies to think of England as very built up. We had a night at Blackpool where we enjoyed strolling around the holiday town, with an overnight stay in one of the many boarding houses available for short stays by holidaymakers. From there we headed to the Lake District and spent some time at Lake Windermere before having a drive around the area. We had lunch by a river near Kendall where we spent time chatting to a group of young campers. We also spent time with some of my friends back at Shaw before I took them back to London in my car.

During the visit they told me that they had booked a trip to head back to Australia using a camping trip on a bus to India as a starting point. The bus was to leave London in October and was planned to take six weeks for the trip. They asked me if I might be interested in joining them so I made a booking as well. When October came around I got a phone call from them to let me know that they had cancelled the trip as they were to stay in London for a while longer. I was primed to return to Australia so I kept my booking intact, mainly because the trip had a planned route which looked too good to miss. So once again it was farewells all around when I set off for London a couple of weeks later.

London

I planned to do this trip to India and then carry on from there overland under my own steam. However, things turned out a bit different after the bus got to Afghanistan, but more of that later. After arriving in London I found my way to the bus departure point, a residential court with an old Bedford bus parked there. A group of people was waiting by the bus, and after handing over the £65 for the cost of the trip it was time to get to know my fellow travellers - 28 including two drivers.

We left from there by about 4 pm and headed for a channel ferry to take us to Belgium. We had been driving for about half an hour or so when the bus decided to take a rest going up a steep hill. We made it a pit stop at a nearby pub called very appropriately if my memory serves me well, The Travellers Rest! A couple of pints later we recommenced the journey only to find that the last ferry for the day had gone, so we spent the first night sleeping on the bus until the first ferry next morning. The upside was it gave us all a chance to get to know each other.

BELGIUM

It was trouble-free driving after arriving in Belgium. The route took us through Brussels and on into Germany with much chatting along the way and no stops other than loo stops and grabbing a bite to eat. There was a rule set here for loo stops out in the countryside which prevailed for the rest of the trip. It was boys to the right side of the bus and girls to the left. By late afternoon we were near the city of Cologne.

Cologne, GERMANY

At Cologne we set up tents at a camping ground, and had a quiet night to be ready for an early start to Munich next day and a visit to the famous beer festival, Oktoberfest. We arrived there in the early afternoon, and once again set up camp at a camping ground on the outskirts of the city. This one was situated by a river which was part of the camp, a pretty good set up with a large raft on the river which had a jazz band on board to entertain the campers for the afternoon and evening. There was no need to go anywhere else with all there was to do at the camp. Although we were all OK with each other there were nonetheless smaller clusters of like-minded people forming within the group. I, myself, had become pretty friendly with a young farmer bloke on his way to Australia for the first time and a girl who was a school teacher on a holiday to India.

The next day we drove into the city, parked the bus and set about doing some sightseeing before meeting at the bus again to make our way to the festival. Parking the bus was no mean feat either with the number of other vehicles trying for the same outcome. It was managed, however, in a spot very close to the festival site. There was plenty of activity around the city with the beer festival being the theme on show of course. One sight to remember was a dray wagon being hauled by two huge horses, with the largest beer barrels imaginable on board. The two guys handling it were dressed in traditional Bavarian clothing and waving to all as they passed by, no doubt on the way to supplying the huge beer halls at the site of the festival.

We spent the afternoon sampling the beers in their huge glasses at the festival. The easiest way to handle these was to pick the glass up using the back of the hand to support the weight through the handle. The waitresses were pretty good at getting the beers to the tables carrying at least three in each hand by the handles, must be quite a knack to that. Very strong these German girls must be. The beer halls were also huge, with hundreds of people in each of them that we visited. After starting out at just after 12 o'clock here I was pleasantly sozzled by mid-afternoon and decided that discretion was the better part of valour and so cut down on my consumption of the amber liquid. We were by now full of chatter after a very enjoyable afternoon. We wandered around the site before we left for the drive back to the camping ground. We left Munich the next day heading for Austria where the main stopping point was to be at Salzburg. It turned out that we did have an overnight stay en route.

AUSTRIA

We spent most of the day after Munich just driving and enjoying the scenery into Austria. We did stop and start a number of times but only for leg stretching, bites to eat and the mandatory loo stops. We spotted a tavern in the early evening so it was agreed that we check it out for a meal. After seeing the meat display for meals being served we decided to stay the night here. I have no idea where we were in terms of a name for the place but back to the meat display. This was indeed a tavern, but it was more like a butchery display. The meal was wonderful, backed up with some good beer to wash it down. We were not in a town but in a small village so some of the hardier ones pitched a tent but it was a very cold night ahead so most of us slept on the bus. It seemed to me that the whole of the village where we were must have used the tavern for dinners as the place was packed to the rafters. Either that or customers came from miles around. Well worth the effort whatever the reasons. The tavern was not open for breakfast so it was a quick wash at a water tap and off along the road to find food.

From there we headed to Salzburg for a two night stay again at a camping ground, meaning we had a full day for sightseeing. We walked around the city, and the small group I was with had an interesting lunch stop. We were just wandering along a street when we heard music coming from a building we were passing, and ventured inside to find a classical music concert in progress. There was no sign of anywhere to pay for admittance so we found seats and stayed for a listen. It went on for about half an hour and then the audience broke up and began partaking of finger food laid out in the hall. We got a rather nice lunch there and never found out what the occasion was. The day we left Salzburg was pretty much a repeat of the day we left Munich with an all-day drive with stops and starts. In fact I guess all our travel days were that format unless being on a stopover somewhere.

YUGOSLAVIA

It was quite late when we got into the city of Belgrade, and the plan was to stop here until morning so we found a large super-market and parked the bus there, so that we could once again use it for sleeping, at least that was the plan. The supermarket shelves were very sparse of anything let alone food items, and it was pretty obvious to all of us that we were now in a pretty poor country. It was decided that as Greece was to be our next planned stopover we would make do with whatever snacks we were able to find and keep going on the road into Greece, keeping a look out for somewhere to eat along the way. We arrived in Greece early next morning and a breakfast stop was high on our agenda.

GREECE

When we found a place to eat we stopped for breakfast then continued south towards our next stopover, a small fishing village called Platamon near Mount Olympus. The next moves after that were to be Daphne and then to Athens. The village turned out to be a real nice one with a camping ground by the beach where we set up camp and spent the day and night there. It was a really good camp with a camp kitchen and very clean showers etc. You could either cook your own food or purchase cooked meals from the owner's canteen. Some bright spark of the group had brought in some goat meat so that was cooked up over an open fire pit and the outcome was just about the worst feed I have ever attempted to eat. Talk about meat packed with bone, it was almost all bones. A bottle of wine and finger food from the canteen helped to fix that.

The next morning when we set about loading up the bus again I thought, *Why not stay here while the bus goes south?* It would have to return this way to continue the trip. So I had a chat to the drivers and told them that I had just recently had a few days in Athens and as this was such a good place, how about I keep a tent with me and stay until they came back past here after Athens? It was to be four days before they were due back so they said there would be no problem if that was what I wanted to do. I was getting a tent from the bus when one of the other guys asked what I was up to and when I told him he thought that he might do the same. It finished up that three of us stayed behind as one of the girls joined us too. She had been one of the quieter people on board so it would be good to get to know her a bit better than I had so far. We were asked to be packed up and ready to go by the morning of the fourth day.

Those days were being spent enjoying the sunshine on the beach, chatting to holidaymakers and enjoying the food on hand at the camp canteen as well as a local restaurant in the village. The cost of what we were doing here was next to nothing with a nice meal and a half bottle of wine coming in at less than $1 a time. The fourth morning came around and we diligently packed our things and put them in a pile while we spent the day around the camp. By late afternoon we figured if they came now, they would stay the night so we set up camp again. This packing up routine went on for a further four or five days before the bus returned. The reason they were late was because the bus was having break-downs and repairs. I guess we got the best of the deal being here at the village. The thing that made us confident that they would return was that for some reason or other some of the bus load had left their passports with the manager of the park until their return, in a cardboard box in his office. Perhaps they had been left as security for payment of the site fee.

A couple of activities we did are worth a mention. One of them resulted from a trip we made up the track towards the top of Mount Olympus, not far from the village. An English guy who had arrived there on holiday with a four wheel drive wagon took us up there. Before we left the camp the girl with us had been sun baking, and decided that her swimming costume would be enough to wear as it was a warm sunny day. I tried to tell her it would be much cooler on the mountain and to have something warm with her but she would have none of that. She did later borrow the jumper I had taken with me.

There was a track for car access which looped up one side of the mountain in a horseshoe shape. The view from a lookout when we stopped was brilliant back down to the coast, and the girl asked me if I would take a couple of movie shots of her on the mountain. She explained to me how her camera operated but I got a little confused. It was a camera with a movie cartridge inside it

92

and when I held the viewing lens to my eye nothing seemed right. It felt very awkward with the trigger button needing to be pressed outwards from my face. Realising then that the camera was back to front in my hands I asked her if she had always used it this way to which she replied that she had. I asked her then how many cartridges had she used and she said five. I then told her it seems that she had five and a half movie films with the camera being used back to front. Oh dear not happy!

Another good day was when the same four of us took a drive down the coast to visit a Greek church which had been built in a rocky hillside and was a local tourist attraction. We were wandering around the site when two buses pulled into the car park, the passengers all got out and began setting up trestle tables and loading them up with food and drinks. We asked two girls what was going on and they told us it was a birthday in the family. They then asked if we were English and would we mind helping them with their English speaking. We were introduced to one of the guys and the result of that was an invitation to share their tables. Wow, that was some party with heaps of this and that food and drinks, and I stuck with the Greek drink Ouzo. I did find it pretty well par for the course for Greek friendliness.

Our bus finally arrived back at the camp site so we were once again on our way to India. We did have a two-night stay at a small village along the coast before carrying on to Turkey. It was at this village that the local young boys spent lots of time on the rocks around the camp's rocky foreshore fishing for small octopus using a broom handle with a nail driven into the end and ground to a sharp point. They would wait for an octopus to move into the shallow water and then push the sharpened baited nail close to its beak whereupon it would take the bait and impale itself on the nail. They would then remove it and slap it around on the rocks before turning it inside out through the beak to clean it out. The catch would be taken home or sold to a small restaurant in the village close by. I had a feed of it there and it was very enjoyable. We left the village early in the morning with a long drive ahead to Istanbul the day after that.

Istanbul, TURKEY

After we entered Turkey we eventually crossed the Bosphorous Strait from Europe to Asia, and booked into a backpackers' hostel very close to the Blue Mosque and the huge ancient monument of Hagia Sophia. Settling into a shared room with three other guys from the bus we switched on the light only to find no action from the light fitting. Well, that's an overstatement as it was just a cord hanging from the ceiling with a light bulb which had a broken filament. I took the bulb down to the reception, basically a hole in the wall with a shelf in front of it, and asked the guy there for a new bulb to put in the room. He went away and came back with a candle, with the comment that it was more romantic! We were there for three nights and with candles for our lighting that would be unacceptable so the manager did find us a light bulb eventually.

Istanbul was a vibrant city with lots of unusual things to see and do. I visited the Blue Mosque and Hagia Sophia as well as a palace approachable only by boat, which was where the sultans had their concubines and eunuchs in days gone by. There were also bazaars to wander around and cottage industries such as gemstone cutting and metal workers with gold, silver and other metals. One guy who obviously had his pitch around the area of the hostel had a bear with a chain around its neck. He was wandering about looking for photo opportunities from any tourists who wanted to take a photo of him and the bear. I explored thoroughly for two full days.

After the delays experienced in Greece it was a quick trip through Turkey after leaving Istanbul with stops along the road for two overnight camps. The first one was by a river where I decided it was a good time to heat a tinned meat pie that I had brought from England. The smell of it on the camp fire drifted around our site and there was a clamour from others to share it. There was a spoonful left for me too afterwards! The next night was a bit different when we did a snack stop at a road side shop where I went for a cold drink. The display cabinet had what I thought were bottles of milk so I ordered one of those. One of these days I will take some notice of vendors in foreign countries who try to talk me out of having what I have ordered. The milk turned out to be one of the most horrible tastes I can remember having in my mouth. Sour as can be and that ended up being thrown away into the nearest garbage bin. The next two interesting stops were in Iran which was the next border to be crossed early the next morning.

IRAN

While Turkey had been a relatively dry landscape with very little greenery (especially the latter part of the journey across the country), Iran was very much the same if not even drier. Our first stop was in the capital city Tehran. It was my birthday that day so a group of us set out to do some celebrating, but in Iran without a pub or two available that was not an easy thing to do. We had to be satisfied with exploring the city streets and nightspots, mainly cafés and coffee shops so not a real lot of excitement with that.

Our next stopover for a couple of days camping again was on the outskirts of the city of Isfahan. We drove into the city for the days with visits to mosques and more cottage industry. Again like Istanbul there were gemstones and metal workers mainly. One interesting visit was to a house where two ladies were weaving a carpet on what must be the oldest weaving loom on the planet. They were using rolls of wool of many colours to make a very nice looking carpet. This being a very poor country meant that it was expected that we give some money for the privilege of watching them at work. I hope they were handsomely paid for the finished article as the work and effort put into the job was 100 per cent with the end product to be a beautiful Persian carpet.

AFGHANISTAN

We crossed the border of Iran into Afghanistan in the late afternoon and were told by the Afghans that camping in the country overnight was not allowed as it was too dangerous with the risk of attacks by bandits. There was an accommodation block at the border compound, and as we were to be here for the night we congregated in a coffee shop of sorts for a bite to eat. The cost of the accommodation had been the equivalent of 10 cents Australian to sleep on the floor. As it was the time of Ramadan the Muslims were not eating until the hours of darkness but that did not present any problems for our group getting food. We stayed at the shop for a few hours as there was nothing else to do at the compound. When darkness came some of the group started to drift off to the sleeping quarters until there was just me and one other guy along with the guy running the shop. He was just about to close up until morning when he offered for us to sleep in his shop for half the cost of the other place so like idiots we took him up on the offer. We got our sleeping bags from across the compound and then went back.

I thought we would be sleeping in the nice warm room but no, he took us through the kitchen area and down two dry earth steps then down onto a similar floor in a room about eight feet square.

He said we could sleep there. There was no lighting but some light did come from the fire pit over which he must have been doing the cooking in his kitchen. It was at this point that we should have had a change of mind but with a little light from the kitchen we stayed. We got into our sleeping bags and within a few minutes an Afghan came down into the room and wrapped himself in a bundle of what looked like old rags in a corner. It took me a while to get to sleep with him there, not knowing quite what to expect. Finally I was asleep when we were woken by a piercing scream in the room. We both leapt out of our sleeping bags and just about got jammed in the doorway trying to get away from whatever it was, then had a good laugh when we saw that it was two cats fighting. Soon after getting back into our bags we were woken again around 4 am by the cooking guy back at work in his kitchen banging pots and pans getting ready for the Muslims at the border post wanting their food before daybreak. We both got our bags and moved across the compound to try to get a bit more sleep before the bus would be ready to leave for the ride to the town of Herat, our next stopover. An old saying is you only get what you pay for, hey!

The ride across to Herat was uneventful, through drab and desolate countryside. We found a backpackers' hostel and stayed in town for the rest of the day and overnight dining mainly on omelettes. I was not game to chance eating meat and kept to food in either a skin to peel off or eggs which had their shell. The houses kept dung stuck onto the walls drying in the sun for use as fuel for the fires which I thought was the ultimate in recycling. One thing that I found interesting to watch was a miller crushing the oil out of nuts and catching it in containers to sell. He had two huge stone circular discs about six inches thick and three feet in diameter placed one on top of the other with the top one being rotated to crush the nuts in the space between them. The oil was collected out of shallow channels at intervals around the lower disc. He had a camel harnessed to the top one as the driving force just walking around in circles to provide the motion. Even for a camel that must be the most boring thing to be doing let alone the guy at the turning stone disc.

The next stop was Kandahar, and we stayed in a big hotel which had only recently been built. The next morning after a nice breakfast, that by the way was a treat long overdue, we left Kandahar heading along the highway to Kabul. The road out of Kandahar was nothing short of brilliant compared to what had been left behind us, with a sealed surface elevated about two feet above the stony desert surrounding it. However, it was not too long before disaster struck, as the driver for some unknown reason suddenly left the road and ran down the rocky sub-surface off the road onto the desert.

That would have been OK, but the bus was confronted by a deep drain dug into the desert for water run-off, about four feet wide and scooped out to a depth of two or three feet. The driver swerved to miss the drain and the bus toppled over onto its side and then onto its roof. It then skidded to a final resting place. The 28 of us on the bus were in various positions with the roof of the bus almost flattened down to the seat tops. I was on the seat second row from the back and with one of the other guys we managed to push out the back window which was not too difficult to remove. Incredibly all 28 of us managed to crawl out of the mangled bus, and even more incredible was the fact that only two of the group had an injury. One guy had a small cut to his scalp and one of the girls had a cut hand which turned out to be the most serious injury.

While we were surveying the damage to the bus and salvaging our luggage and stuff which belonged to the owners such as the camping equipment, a group of men came out of nowhere on horseback and parked themselves about 30 metres away just watching what we were doing. We had a meeting of sorts to think

98

of what to do next. It was decided that half a dozen of the guys would stay at the scene while the rest made their way into Kabul one way or another. A short time later a local bus came along the road on its way to Kabul so most of the group were able to find seats on that, including me. The rest stayed with the bus and we reported the accident to the British Consul at Kabul and asked for help to be sent to the ones still with the bus.

Kabul, AFGHANISTAN

A couple of the guys went to find the British Embassy, and the consul asked for a rundown on the happening. When he heard the name of the tour company he said that there was already a bus belonging to them in the compound of the embassy awaiting the owners to collect it following the last tour that they had run to the city. Apparently it was to be collected when this tour was passing through Kabul on the way to India. Not the best of an outcome for the owners by the sound of all that, if indeed a true story. It seemed hard to believe, but perhaps I should just take some things at face value. Help would soon be on its way and that was the last I saw of the tour group as we all went our separate ways from there. I stayed at Kabul for two or three days and visited the hospital to see how the girl with the injured hand was. I found out that she had been in surgery for attention to it. The group sort of just filtered away with some backtracking to England and others going forward to their own destinations.

There was one day there at Kabul when I found a market on my wanderings, with a snake charmer doing his stuff with a cobra in a basket. He was attracting quite a crowd of locals with his flute causing the snake to rise up and down from the basket, and motioned for me to go over to him but I was not game to get involved in any of his efforts to include me in his act so I politely refused. There was a bus to leave Kabul for the Pakistan border and another bus from there which continued on through the Khyber Pass which was quite an experience. The Pass would have seen many a sight over the years, and figures in many tales of the East. After negotiating the Pass the city of Peshawar was only a short distance from there, and I stayed here overnight at a back-packers' hostel ready to catch a train into India.

Peshawar, PAKISTAN

The day after arriving at Peshawar I got onto a train to India, having considered my options overnight. The train went first to Amritsar and then another one on to New Delhi. It had been my decision to head straight to Australia from New Delhi rather than slowly making my way there via some of the Far Eastern countries. I would leave all that until a later date after my next stint working the country jobs in Australia. The new plan would be to end that trip at New Delhi when I could take a little longer perhaps to see the sights before flying out of there to England.

New Delhi, INDIA

After a couple of days having a little break and absorbing the culture on view in the city I got a flight to Darwin in the Northern Territory via Hong Kong. The most eventful moment on that flight was the landing at the Hong Kong airport which was really part of the city centre jutting out into the harbour. The aircraft had to literally drop from the sky after clearing the city skyscrapers in order to get onto the runway, pretty much a frightening experience. There were a few hours to kill before the connecting flight so I was given a transit visa to cover the time which enabled me to take a look around the city, just outside the airport exit and within walking distance.

Darwin, NT, AUSTRALIA

I had been having a great time for the past eight weeks or so on the trip so I decided that the best thing for me to do was to try to get a country job to fund my next trip, whenever that may be. I did not mess around here and went to the Commonwealth Employment Service building to see what might be available. I had spent some time in Darwin on my previous visit to the Northern Territory so there was no point in waiting. The consultant almost dragged me over the counter when I said that I was an electrician looking for country work. He said that there was a project in Arnhem Land 400 miles or so to the east where a bauxite mine and new town were being developed. This was at a place called Gove and the new town would be named Nhulunbuy. I was hired by the building company there and was flown out the next day.

Nhulunbuy, NT

The flight over Arnhem Land was quite spectacular with dense vegetation interacting with deep gorges and waterfalls along the way. Part of this area has since opened up to tourism with the establishment of the large Kakadu National Park. How different this scenery was compared to the countryside of Iran and Afghanistan, those being a sort of grey colour and so little greenery.

It was getting close to Christmas when I arrived at Gove and was delegated a job looking after repairs to power tools for the company. I found this rather boring and after talking it over with the boss he organised a job for me with the company installing the refrigeration and air conditioning for the new town of Nhulunbuy. I was to remain in this job for about a year before venturing away again on my travels. The couple of weeks left to go before Christmas and New Year were spent trying to get used to the climate and the drastic change in lifestyle, working ten-hour days again for six days a week. Accommodation was in a block of rooms with about 12 rooms to a block. This was also a big change because all the rooms here were for two sharing in the same one, and I got to know a few different co-habitants in this way.

One of the first things to happen in my new job was that I met up with the ute driver from Adelong again, the ute I almost froze in while riding in the cargo tray that first morning there. He was working for the same company that I had joined. At first sight I did not realise it was him, and it was only when he recognised me from the Tumut job that we realised that we already knew each other. By now he had grown a beard so I had not known it was him until then. It was a small crew of electricians working for the company with only one other besides us and the supervisor.

1971

Early in the New Year at Nhulunbuy brought another reunion with my good mate from the Exmouth days, who had visited me at my parents' house a few months ago. He and his travelling companion who had also worked at Exmouth both turned up here at Nhulunbuy, so there were some good times ahead with stories of our travels over a beer or two.

One of the best things we did here was to go out to a beach one Saturday afternoon after work, have a campfire meal and sleep under the stars. There was a group of about 25 piled into one of the work trucks as well as a couple of 4x4s and we drove through the bush to the beach. We arrived at the beach and unloaded the truck of sleeping bags and blankets as well as a good supply of liquid refreshment. There was also a long net for catching fish for the meal. We laid the net out along the beach and it turned out to be about 30 metres in length and a width of about a metre. A group of us spaced ourselves along its length about two metres apart. Picking up the net we then walked into the sea following tentatively onward in the footsteps of the leading bloke. The net was now about 20 metres out forming an arc out into the sea. We stretched it to its full length and it was during this activity that I became very wary of where my feet were treading. Unable to swim, and with the water above my waist, I was more than a little nervous. Thankfully I did not have a problem as the sandy bottom was firm and trouble free. When the net had been walked back to the beach it revealed quite an assortment of fish, which we sorted and either kept or put back in the sea. We did this two or three times and caught enough for a meal for everyone. We made a fire and enjoyed a good night.

I guess this is not the time, being so late after the event, but I can't help thinking of the danger we put ourselves into. The danger was very real, with the knowledge I now have of the plentiful numbers of huge salt water crocodiles in the waters around the top end of the country. Ignorance is bliss according to an old saying and I guess that was true. It is not uncommon to hear of people being taken by the crocodiles up there.

There was one awesome sight in the new town site one Saturday when I was driving to a particular job in the ute, passing the power station which was by now operative. The high tension power lines from there were run overhead across the roadway and a truck with an extended crane on the back accidentally ran the crane into the power lines. As this happened there was a very loud bang and a flash with all the tyres on the truck instantly bursting into flames. The driver should have had an instant reaction to lift his feet up and get into a squatting position on the driving seat and I hope he did do that until it was safe for him to get out of the truck. Bystanders rushed over to the truck immediately.

Midway through my time here saw the completion of the Walk-about Hotel, which would make a nice change from having a few beers at the wet canteen on site when it opened for business. The hotel had been given Priority One. There had been a miscalculation however, and by the looks of things the licence to operate had been refused because there was no operating police station built in the town as yet. The nearest police station was a 400 mile flight away in Darwin of course. It was amazing, the speed that a police station could be built and manned. I reckon it was a three-week turnaround from nothing to operating, with tradesmen like flies buzzing around getting on with that job. The wet canteen did keep on running and it was a lot easier to get to even if the hotel was open, so just for a bit of a change was all that I used that for.

The facility for meals here was a huge mess hall with a kitchen area open for all to see, and the serving bar and bain marie had an open front looking into the kitchen. The three daily meals always had at least three choices and mixing up the various choices was OK if desired, almost a smorgasbord really. There was a commotion or two with some workers not happy with what they were offered, a bit unfair in my book, as I thought the food was pretty good. Whenever those occasions did occur, few and far between I might add, the security staff were always very quick to respond. These times invariably were the outcome of just how living in the tropics can have an effect on some people. Here it was called Going Troppo, maybe that is a common colloquialism.

The time came when my Adelong mate decided he would go home to Germany for a holiday so off he went. After a few weeks he returned to the site so we carried on with our work but only for a few more weeks. He had met a German lass while on holiday and so he decided to return to Germany to be with her. Our supervisor organised a farewell party for him after work to be held in the wet canteen on the day before he left. All the guys on the air conditioning crew who he had worked alongside for the last couple of years were invited.

My mate was given the afternoon off work to do his packing, and we started to congregate in the wet canteen for the party. My supervisor, the other electrician and I had an early knock off to have a couple of quiet drinks before the rest of the crew turned up. At this point I should mention that all the time that my mate had been here he had a beard, a fairly long wispy beard. My days at Adelong with him back in 1966 had seen him clean-shaven, showing his noticeably receding chin. I was reminded of this when he came to join us at the wet canteen, as he had shaved his beard off and he was a totally different person to look at. Our supervisor had a good sense of humour and when he saw this he said not to say anything to the others when they started to arrive. He then proceeded to introduce him to all and sundry as the new sparky who was the replacement electrician. Believe it or not each and every one of them shook hands with him until he could not keep his laughter under wraps any longer. The other guys just could not believe the change which no beard had made to him. Anyway, he went on his merry way next day and that was the last I saw or heard from him. He had been a real good workmate.

A time came when I had a room to myself, but not for long as a young bloke who had been working in Canada came and took over the spare side of the room. He was from New Zealand and had some good tales of his job and visit in Canada. On his first day he produced a pair of really good quality work boots which were brand new and he asked me if it was practice to leave boots out in the corridor at night. He had seen how everyone did this and was a bit doubtful about leaving his there. The reason for that, I told him, was to keep the smell of the boots out of the rooms and as far as I knew the boots were quite safe to be left there. Thinking about that I should have kept my mouth closed because after the first night of him doing that there were no boots outside our door other than my grubby old ones. He was not too happy, I can tell you.

As the weeks passed I started to get itchy feet once again as the travel bug started to bite. It was this frame of mind that saw me leave Nhulunbuy after a very enjoyable time. My boss gave me a ride to the airstrip and I boarded the daily flight which serviced Nhulunbuy from Darwin, to leave Arnhem Land behind.

Darwin, NT

It was a long trip from Darwin to Sydney and for starters I booked a bus to Brisbane. The drive was via the small town of

Katherine with a brief stop at Daly Waters before changing buses at the Three Ways just north of Tennant Creek, covering just short of 1000 kilometres so far. It would be generous if I put Katherine town itself any more than three kilometres from end to end and Daly Waters was nothing more than a pub for all intents and purposes. The Three Ways was just a roadhouse for fuel and food. This was a good cameo of what makes Australia such a unique country and one of the reasons why I was enjoying living and working here so much. Plenty of wide open spaces with the large towns and cities pleasantly spaced within.

With another 3000 kilometres to go before getting to Sydney I settled down for a day or two on the bus. The next stop was Mount Isa which awakened memories of the last time I had travelled this road with the breakdown of the bus and the ensuing situation. No such occurrence this time around. The ride from Mount Isa to Townsville was largely over still unsealed road and the corrugations in the gravel surface made resting comfortably a non-event. It was a real bone shaker for a large part of the ride. The sealing of this highway was not finished until 1976.

Townsville, QLD

As I had previously passed through Townsville only briefly for a visit I decided to stay over for a couple of days for a look around the city. It was not a large place but had a nice beach, very accessible and close to the city centre. I did a good steep walk up to the lookout on Castle Hill, with sweeping views of nearby Magnetic Island and further out to sea, as well as across the city. I figured that this might be a good place to come and live for a while sometime, maybe in the future.

I continued southward by bus again to Brisbane, breaking my journey for a couple of nights at Noosa Heads for the same reason as my stay at Townsville. Noosa was a small village at this time, but has since developed into a premier tourist resort. It was good to experience the town as it was pre the boom days, very laid back and quiet. Resuming the journey on to Brisbane by bus I then converted my mode of transport to the train for the trip down south to Sydney.

Sydney, NSW

After having a few days with my mates at Sydney I decided to have a trip back to England to spend Christmas and New Year with my family. Having travelled on the ship/jet tour last time it seemed like a good idea to put a tour of my own together so I went ahead with that plan. I visited a travel agency and booked on a P&O cruise which was sailing from Sydney to Singapore, then I would leave the cruise at Singapore and connect with a flight to London with a budget carrier airline. With this booking now in place I spent a few more days in Sydney until the departure day came along.

Back in Nhulunbuy one of the other electricians I had worked with gave me his home phone number in Melbourne, and as the ship had a stop there I phoned him to see if it might be possible to catch up. He responded very positively by saying that he and another of the electricians who had also been at Nhulunbuy would meet me at the port and have a few drinks around town. That was something to look forward to.

Sydney to Singapore

The trip to Melbourne from Sydney took a couple of days and upon docking at the port, there at the dockside were my two ex-workmates. It was late in the afternoon, with a departure time of 11pm later that night. We had a great time doing a grand tour of the pubs and bars around the city centre. I caught a taxi back to the ship and was back on board in good time, and the two friends and I went our different ways.

The next port to visit was Fremantle; however, an unscheduled stop was made off-shore near Albany in Western Australia to allow the police to board the ship from a tender craft. During the night the bank office on board had been broken into and a large sum of money had been stolen. The police made extensive enquiries around the passengers, staying on board for that while the ship continued with the journey. It became knowledge that a lifebelt was missing so the opinions were that the money had been tied to that and thrown overboard for someone to collect from shore in a small boat. That sure was an outrageous crime anyway, whatever way it was done.

My time at Fremantle was spent strolling around the town. From Fremantle the next stop was the Island of Penang off the Malaysian west coast. Here I went ashore with one of the guys who shared my four-berth cabin. We arrived there mid-morning and were to leave for the next stop at Kuala Lumpur at 11 pm. We spent the day looking at some of the tourist attractions including a visit to the Snake Temple, where there were lots of snakes all lying in states of repose. I reckon all the burning joss sticks were the reason for that. Anyway one of the attendants asked if we would like the poisonous vipers placed upon our heads for a photo. My mate refused but I thought *Why not?* So I allowed him to place a handful of them there. Do not ask why I did that; it must have been a brain explosion probably.

As evening came we found ourselves in a bar where two of the crew were also having some shore leave. We had the rest of the time together with them before one of us realised the time had got away, and made a bee line for rickshaws to get us back to the ship before it left us behind. Unfortunately that is exactly what it did do. There the four of us were on the dockside with the ship about 30 metres away setting sail. A man came rushing over to us, who turned out to be the agent at Penang for the cruise and he told us to wait where we were for him to come back. He did come back but it was in a small boat which he told us to get into and then he took off chasing the ship in an effort to catch up to it. He gave up after a few minutes, as the ship was obviously at too high a speed for him to get near. It was doubtful if I was pleased or sorry about that as I did wonder how we would get aboard if he did catch up to it. Anyway, he turned the boat around, none too happy, and took us back to the dockside and from there it was a taxi to the Seaman's Mission at Penang for a night's sleep and breakfast the next morning. From there we caught a taxi to the airport and collected tickets for a flight to Kuala Lumpur. A taxi was ordered there to take us to the ship. I asked the agent how much all of that was to cost and he told me to go see the purser on the ship when we got back on board to fix that up. It was with bated breath that I approached the purser and was so relieved when the sum total for all of that came to $18 only.

Kuala Lumpur, MALAYSIA

After the events just gone by I did not go ashore here but just spent the time lazing around and counting my blessings at getting off with what had happened so well. The next stop was Singapore and after negotiating a very crowded harbour the ship docked at the port and I was at the end of this particular part of the journey.

SINGAPORE

This was my second time in Singapore, the first being a short transit stop at the airport on the flight to Sydney in 1966 when I emigrated. It had been so hot and steamy then, even though the time had been about 11 pm, but this time I was prepared, with more appropriate clothing. There were arrangements already made at a hotel for a couple of days' stopover to take in a few of the sights and get a real feel for being there. I had a good look around the city and enjoyed sampling the variety of foods from the vendors, particularly at Chinatown and Orchard Road.

It was now close to Christmas and I boarded my flight to London ready for a good time with my family and friends once again back at Shaw. In London I found my way to Euston railway station for the train ride to Manchester. From there it was a bus to Shaw. Christmas was a good time with a big party at my parents' house on Christmas Eve.

1972

Shaw, ENGLAND

It was the working factor which made my mind up once again to just have a nice time with my family and friends for a couple of months, then back to Aussie. The work I found was a casual job in one of the cotton mills in Shaw, and they are not the best of environments to be in all day; humid and a little musty from the cotton being processed. Unfortunately these mills have now ceased to be, as the industry has all but gone with a few of the mills now converted to warehouses or let as small manufacturing workshops, as I discovered on a holiday to Shaw late in 2013.There would have been ten of them around the town back in the 70s but now there are only two or three still standing, with the others having been demolished, including the one that I worked in at the time of my visit.

By March I was ready to organise my next trip to Australia, and found a travel agency with a Russian ship due to sail from Singapore to Fremantle in the middle of March. I booked a passage, and also a seat with a budget airline from London to Singapore, leaving myself a couple of days stopover before the ship sailed. When the time came to leave Shaw I bade my farewells once again to everyone and went by train to London.

London

I did not spend any more time in London than I needed, and made my way to my bank in the city to check that the balance would be available for me at a branch in Perth when I arrived there. From there it was a trip to Gatwick airport for my flight to Singapore.

SINGAPORE

I enjoyed a couple of days in Singapore again, including a promised-to-myself brief visit to the Raffles Hotel to mix with the upper crust. When I got there I found a nice quiet lounge, very cool and tropical looking. Sitting in such an old-world environment was very pleasant. It was just as enjoyable, however, mixing with the street foodies once again on Orchard Road sampling the food there. It was a nice interlude though.

It was then onto the high seas on the Russian ship and what a boring sail that was. No activities at all on board but the bars were open, thank goodness. Not the ideal cruise but it served the purpose of getting me back to Australia, with Fremantle turning on a nice sunny welcome.

Perth, WA

I made my way into Perth ready to seek employment. All it took was a phone book and a pocket full of coins in a phone box, and a ring around looking for country jobs. I nailed one for Cape Lambert 1600 kilometres north of Perth on the coast. The work was on a new plant being constructed to turn the iron ore from the Pilbara region into pellets ready for export to Asian countries.

Cape Lambert, WA

The departure from the aircraft at Dampier airport was memorable, as the dry heat hit me in the face at the exit door. The best comparison I can use is that it was as if someone had opened an oven door when roasting meat. Coming straight from Singapore where the heat had been just the opposite, hot, humid and sticky at least until the evenings, was probably one reason why it affected me so. And added to that of course I had been thrown into that pretty much straight from the cold and wintry conditions in Shaw!

Cape Lambert was one of the quietest places I lived in. There was a wet canteen on site but I did not use it much as I spent the first week or two getting my bank balance looking a bit like healthy again. There was a pub in Roebourne, the nearest town, and I did just a couple of Sunday trips there. The site was right by the sea so we did get some nice cooling breezes now and then with the opposite side of the site being an expanse of dry sparsely vegetated bush.

One day the foreman took me up to the top of two or three ore bins which had been recently built, to size up the job of installing lights up there. We climbed the steps up to the walkways across the top of them and were now at a good height from ground level to take in the views around us. As we got to the top the foreman said to me what a good view it was from up there.

Doing a 360 degree panorama of it I answered him with, "Well, if you mean you can see a long way, well then, yes it is."

The view was of the ocean on one side and as I rotated, the bush took over as far as the now very distant horizon of reddish brown earth with the sparse bushes dotted about here and there. The only town I can recall seeing was either Dampier or Roebourne in the distance along the coast within that entire expanse. It had further impressed on me the vastness of Australia and the bare minimum of people making it their home, especially in these remote regions.

It was here that I came across another English electrician who became a good friend and joined my Sydney group of mates. I was to stay here on the job at Cape Lambert for a short time only and early in May I left to go to Perth for a while. I had saved well here so I was ready for moving on again. I had enjoyed my time in Perth last time so that is where I went to. So it was back to Dampier and then a flight to Perth.

Perth, WA

My first objective was to find some accommodation, a guest house which had short term rental. I chanced my arm at getting employment with the pocket full of coins in a phone box again which had been a successful way of gaining a job previously. Once again it worked for me, ending up with a job working for a city contractor. So I was set up for a good time here living and working close to the city centre and its attractions.

I stayed for the better part of two months on jobs in and around the city with my weekends spent exploring the many daytime attractions that Perth has, and also trying out the night life. After a few weeks of this I saw the electrician from Cape Lambert with one of the others from the site. He told me that they were on the way to Sydney on the train the next day going via Adelaide and then Melbourne. We went for a few beers that night which is when I made my mind up to travel with them. That meant a phone call to work next morning to tell them I was bailing out to go to Sydney as the train left in the mid-morning. They were OK about it and asked about my pay and tools. I told them to forward my pay to me care of the General Post Office at Martin Place in Sydney, which I had used on other occasions when in Sydney. As I only had what I called a survival kit of tools I said to let anyone who wanted them to just have them.

Sydney, NSW

The trip to Sydney did not eventuate to be all the way by train. We took the train from Perth to Port Augusta in South Australia and from there a train continued on to Adelaide, and it was bus travel from there, first to Melbourne and then on to Sydney. The train across the Nullarbor Plain was now the Indian Pacific, a fairly new train which connected Perth with Sydney and also by virtue of its name the two oceans by a direct route, with the change of trains at Kalgoorlie no longer being done. A bit of a shame, as I would have enjoyed another ride on the old train I had used last time. So, it was a change of trains at Port Augusta to take us to Adelaide.

The bus ride from Adelaide to Melbourne was uneventful, and in the bus station at Melbourne we were waiting around before being allowed to board the bus now manoeuvring into position. Suddenly I saw a bag on the floor just as a wheel of the bus passed over it, and thought I recognised it as the bag that my mate had been carrying with him. When I pointed this out to him his reply amused me when he said that his was like that one but his was much fatter. Then I told him that the bus had just run over it, and he got into a bit of a flap. I suggested he go to report the incident and yes it was his bag with a cassette player shattered within it. He did in due course receive some compensation with a cheque far higher in value than what was originally in the bag, so he was happy about that. That was not the end of the day however,
116

because when the bus got to Sydney it was quite late, around 10 pm. We went to a guest house nearby and booked a room for the night as it was a bit late to go to find mates at that time. We dropped our bags into the room while we went out for a drink before calling it a day.

When we got back to the room we found that the door had been broken open, and the room was in a bit of a mess with our bags having been ransacked. The manager called the police but they did not give us hope of getting our stuff back that was stolen. My camera had gone but the main thing missing was my leather folder which contained all my work references and trade papers. It was a lucky break for me when they were found in a rubbish bin at the guest house just a short time after the cleaners started work next morning. All were there, though mixed up a bit. Also, I was glad that I had my bank passbook with me that night so no money was lost either.

Next morning we left the guest house and went to seek out my mates over the other side of the harbour bridge. There was not enough room with them for three imports so we found a guest house almost within shouting distance of the place where they were living and took a month's booking there. My old mates were all there if scattered about a little so there were a few good times ahead of us. While I was checking the job adverts in the Sydney Morning Herald I found that a major hotel in Sydney was looking for maintenance workers including electricians. After a phone call to them I turned up for an interview for a position to find myself sitting waiting with three other guys for the same job. I was the only one there on the following Monday to start work after being the successful one, so I was thankful for that.

While I worked here I got myself an electrician's licence for working in New South Wales. My documentation from England along with the licences I now had from Queensland and Western Australia was enough to qualify for a NSW one.

Soon it was early autumn, and I figured it would be good to take a short holiday so I chose to do a cruise to some of the Pacific islands. There were P&O liners doing them at the time so I booked myself on one to visit Auckland in New Zealand, Fiji, Tonga and Port Vila, capital of Vanuatu which was then called The New Hebrides. None of the other mates wanted to join me so I went solo but a shipload of mainly young holidaymakers meant ready-made fun.

NEW ZEALAND

In New Zealand I did a bus tour out of Auckland to a town populated mainly by the Maori inhabitants, called Rotorua. It was really interesting to see how the people led their lives in days gone by with activities going on especially to show the tourists how things were - and still are in lots of situations. The town is set within a region of high thermal activity with steam erupting through fissures in the ground from far below. There are pools of hot spring water and even some areas of boiling mud. We were shown how these could be used for cooking purposes with nicely cooked food being the outcome. A strong smell of sulphur was evident within the town as well as near the steam eruptions. We were also taken to two lakes in the craters of supposedly extinct volcanoes, but with all the other thermal activity going on in the region, extinct is a fact that I would be inclined to doubt. The strange thing about these lakes was that one was vibrant blue and the other a distinct green colour. The belief is that the high mineral content of the area has a lot to do with the colouring of the lakes. There are also many Maori myths and legends as to the cause.

FIJI

We docked at Suva and I accompanied another passenger ashore who had invited me to spend the day on a visit to her brother and family who lived on the island. He was a minister of religion, at a village somewhere in the interior of the island and a very interesting day it was, starting with a fairly long drive to the village. Here we were given a really nice lunch by the family and a tour of the village where he plied his trade so to speak. I cannot remember which religion he was, but he did have a small church there. The area was lush with vegetation and very hot and humid after the sea air enjoyed on board the ship. The family got us back to the ship well in time for us to continue on with the cruise. Tonga was the next island ahead of us so it was somewhere new once again to look forward to.

TONGA

At Tonga I spent the day lounging on a beach and checking out the many souvenir stalls that were set up for the tourists. I was a typical Pom as the Aussie saying goes, with short arms and long pockets, spending very little! There were lots of baskets and hats on tables and some laid out on matting on the ground, all made from a grass-like material after many hours' work. Another place that passengers went to see was the Royal Palace which looked to me not much grander than a classy weatherboard house back in Australia, nicely painted and obviously well looked after, with real nice gardens, but not what I expected of a palace. The palace itself would look quite at home in Australia where classic weatherboard houses are built.

Port Vila, VANUATU

The last stop was Port Vila and my time there was spent exploring around the town and sampling the local beverages. The trip back to Sydney from there was much better than the last time I sailed on the Tasman Sea, with no bad weather. The holiday ended back at Sydney so it was then back to work.

Not long after the cruise I left from the hotel job to get back into construction, as the job here had become a bit repetitive and a change was on the cards.

Sydney, NSW

It only took a short while to find the job I was looking for, when I wandered into a new high rise building in the process of being built. I got a job on the site after a chat with the electrician on the job. After a trip across the bridge to the company office for an interview I was to spend the rest of the year working on that building. There were only two electricians and it was here I worked with probably the most meticulous electrician I ever came across. For every one of the fifteen or so levels he drew scale plans of every conduit laying in the concrete pours and we fitted anchors for the fluorescent lights in the car park levels as we went. Simply a threaded insert into a socket nailed into the form work which was removed after the concrete had set. The insert was exposed and just needed to be removed for the light fitting anchor points. Very ingenious I thought. It was to save a lot of time drilling for the anchor points at fitting off.

In the public bar of my local hotel one afternoon I spied my mate from Nhulunbuy, the same one who had worked with me at Exmouth and visited my parents' house in England a couple of

120

years previously. That hotel had by now become the first place to look in Sydney to catch up with the guys who had developed into a group of good mates. We enjoyed nights out, some best forgotten, into the small hours of the morning in the night clubs of Kings Cross, the epicentre of the city's night life.

The first Tuesday in November, the horse race that stops the nation, the race of all races in Australia, the Melbourne Cup is run. Most people would be stopping work to either find a TV set or radio to watch or listen to it. My boss and I went down the street to a hotel to watch in the bar, and it was there that I got my first notion of Tasmania. It was a little-known outside Tasmanian chance of a horse called Piping Lane that won, causing quite a commotion nation-wide. Tasmania was known then as just a little backwater and to some extent that is much the case today. However, many mainlanders are pleasantly surprised at the diversity that the island offers without the large distances sometimes involved on the mainland. I have lived here for many years now in the island state, enjoying its many pursuits.

Anyway as the end of the year approached I was starting to get itchy feet again and looking to do some more travelling in the New Year.

1973

Christmas and the better part of January was spent enjoying time off work at the multi-storey building so when I returned after the holiday break I told my boss that I wanted to do some more travelling and would therefore be leaving Sydney for a while. He was understanding about this and said he was not at all surprised from the way I had been going on about the joy of travelling while I had been working alongside him. Soon after that I left to go once again into the Northern Territory, to Tennant Creek working for a major electrical contracting company on a mine site and then onward to Darwin as a stepping off point for the continent. I flew to Tennant Creek, on my way once again to new pastures on my new job; however, the place I went to east of the town was anything but pastures, with plenty of outback dust and very little vegetation.

Tennant Creek, NT

I was transported to the mine site about an hour's drive out of the town, not quite the moonscape of the ride in to Mt Goldsworthy in Western Australia but dry and dusty all the same. The job was the building of an extraction plant to recover the gold from the ore body taken from the mine. There was a supervisor on site and a crew of 20 other electricians and fitter welders. The billeting was in one of the single rooms which thankfully were clean and comfortable. It was a mixed bag of nationalities on site with Australia, England, Ireland and South Africa all represented in the crew. We became good friends and were to discover that a similar crew was working for the same company on a smelter also being constructed about 10 miles towards town. The guys at that site were to become major contributors to the entertainment with some good Sunday cricket matches, a boxing night and table tennis. I was here for only six weeks, which was when the cricket matches came to an abrupt halt, at least as far as our little group of cricketers was concerned.

The table tennis night was held in the wet canteen at the smelter site, a rectangular building made of wooden posts with a tin roof and four low walls of hessian cloth. These walls only extended four feet from the ground, with rails supporting the hessian around the perimeter, the space above open to the outside for ventilation. An open doorway allowed access to the interior. The only wall from floor to roof was where a bar was situated along the wall, and there were some chairs and tables. The open aspect was good for relief from the daytime heat but was a nuisance when the sun went down and the lights switched on, with hundreds of insects attracted to the lights. The worst ones were the flying ants. We were there for table tennis meaning the bats came in handy for keeping the flying ants at bay. That became more of a sport than the table tennis; however, it had been worth going there if only for the beer!

There was a Sunday boxing competition organised and once again our group of guys who made up the cricket team went along with a few others on the crew. There were two South African guys working with us, one in his early 20s and the other in mid 30s. The younger one had a fiery temperament but the older one kept a tight rein on him as needed. My bout was with the older one and did not last the first round unfortunately, or should that be fortunately? The latter I think, as a good solid punch to the side of my head sent me into a spin and that was the end of that bout. The only other time I can recall being in a boxing ring was in the gym in my school days and that did not last much longer as I recall. Boxing is not really my forte I presume.

While on the subject of punch-ups, one day a group of us decided to take the day off and go into town at Tennant Creek to check out the two pubs, and we soon settled into one. It was crowded with people, both white and aboriginal. Games of 8-ball were in full swing and the young South African was playing against one of the others in our group. A friendly argument broke out between them and the South African swung his cue over his head in mock battle but the problem was a young aboriginal guy was right behind him and the thick end of the cue smacked down hard on his skull sending him crashing to the floor. A massive brawl broke out with people throwing punches willy-nilly. It did not last long however, as I reckon the bar staff must have had a panic button in contact with the police as the pub was soon invaded by the police to put a stop to the melee. Thankfully, I managed to end the day in one piece.

The cricket matches were well organised and a good time was had by everyone. That was only on three occasions unfortunately. They were played on some level ground by the smelter site with no grass, just a dusty expanse of reddish ground for the pitch. After the first two it was one win apiece and a good few beers in the wet canteen, but the fun was too good to last.

Arrangements had been made for our crew to work on the Sunday of that week but the Saturday night at the mine site wet canteen saw a change of plan. We decided that the cricket match, which was now considered a regular activity, took precedence over working for the day. So, work was forgotten on Sunday.

On Monday morning we were all told to sit in the site shed where the boss turned up for a little chat with those who had not turned up for work on Sunday. He handed out pay packets with final pays including the value of a one way air ticket back to the place of employment. There was an hour to pack our stuff before we were taken into Tennant Creek on the bus run.

I used my pay to get started on my way overseas, with the bus to Darwin to get the ball rolling.

Darwin, NT

After arriving in Darwin I had a couple of nights in a motel in the city before going to the offices of the Commonwealth Employment Service, the main providers of work here. The reception clerk just about dragged me in when I said I was an electrician looking for work! This must have been normal procedure here when a tradesman rocked up. She produced a long cardboard box crammed with small cards stacked one against the other, containing job information. How times have changed with jobs just about 10 a penny then, as the saying goes.

The one I chose was a small company in the city, small being the operative word as the man I saw was the owner, and no signs of anyone else. He hired me anyway and took me into the CBD to look at a job for floodlighting a shop window in a new concrete building there. After making a note of any materials needed he drove me back to his workshop, gave me keys for a van parked there and left me to get organised. First problem was to find a step ladder, as the only one there was an old wooden one with a few of the staves still on it, wobbled like crazy too. Next problem was finding a hammer drill for drilling into the concrete, no luck there either; only an old, what used to be called, belly-buster, cast iron, heavy and with no hammer function. Next problem was drills and screws, with just a drawer in an old bench containing an assortment of old and rusty screws. At this point I decided it was time for a chat with the boss. When I pointed out the condition of his equipment all he said was that he had managed alright with the gear he had. My reply was that we were wasting our time if that was how things were to be. I just told him that and left. I went

125

back to the CES and the same clerk said that I was back soon. After I explained what had transpired she got the file box again and found me a casual job on the street lighting in the city.

With a job organised I worked at preparing for my next trip overseas. I planned to do the overland trip I had done from London, in reverse with the intention of visiting the countries I had skirted last time due to budget limitations. I would go overland to India then fly to London from there. To keep myself occupied in Darwin I spent Saturday afternoons at the horse races honing my skills as a punter. It was all to no avail, but I kept my nose in front so to speak and did not get into any losing streaks. I found it enlightening to see how the Territory people actually enjoyed having a punch-up outside the hotels. It seemed the local population took this as normal but I steered a path around such goings on.

This was prior to Cyclone Tracy which hit Darwin in 1974 and the architecture of the city was quite unique at this time. Many-posted verandahs and ornamental railings around upper levels of buildings made the city visually interesting. It was on one of these verandahs at a motel which I had previously stayed at that I watched totally spellbound, the electrical storm out over the sea. A sight never forgotten.

One amusing incident while doing the street lighting was a drive for the two of us down the highway to the small settlement of Humpty Doo south of Darwin. The report was that the light in the phone box at the post office was not working. We did the 40 kilometre drive there to find that it was only the light bulb needing changing. A long way to do just that, but I guess the boss was playing safe by sending the two of us down there. There was a nice break on the way back however, when we stopped at Howard Springs, a nice shady spot by a billabong just off the highway.

The time came for me to set in motion my trip, booking a flight to Timor to the north of Darwin. My journey as far as New Delhi would take about four weeks, so I got a month's supply of malaria pills for travelling through the tropics but as it turned out I should have got more. Of course when I eventually got to New Delhi I then decided to just keep going the way I had been up to that point.

TIMOR

Timor is fairly close to Darwin so after a short flight I arrived at Bacau in East Timor. My first challenge was to get to Indonesian Timor to the west. The eastern part of the island was governed by Portugal. The manager of a backpackers' hostel told me that I must first get to Dili, the capital of East Timor. We got chatting at the small bar over a couple of bottles of beer and he pointed out to me where I could get what he called a bus to go to Dili, which I caught the following day.

The 'bus' turned out to be an old five tonne truck with a canvas cover on the back for shelter and a bench down each side. The passengers were a mixture of locals, a couple of goats and just me as the only foreign-looking person on board. The trip took three to four hours and one of the most significant things on the way was everyone having to get off the truck while it forded across a pretty wide river, probably 40 metres to wade carrying my backpack. Unable to swim, I made sure I kept close behind someone else. I was beginning to regret never getting the hang of swimming and had no choice but to go for the wading. I was relieved to get to the other side. The ride itself was very bumpy and because of the canvas cover I was only able to see out of the back at the passing scenery. What I could see was pretty lush vegetation and the rivers were crystal clear flowing in mountainous surroundings.

127

At Dili the truck dropped everyone off at the market place where I discovered accommodation for backpackers at the beach, affectionately named "The Hippie Hilton" by previous backpackers. My planned four week trip started to stretch out a bit here; at 50 cents a day it was well worth staying on for a few more days than I had anticipated. At the rear of the beach was a three-sided structure facing the sea with a tin roof for cover. Once inside looking out of the open front, I was able to step directly onto the beach. It had ample space with no internal walls other than for a toilet on one side and a shower on the other, the floor was concrete with a scattering of sleeping bags and backpacks. Outside the front was a shallow fire pit scooped out of the beach for cooking and heating, with a constant supply of wood.

Anyone using the facility had no fear of their backpacks being raided with the caretakers, employees of the city council, there all day keeping watch. After settling in I got to looking around the town, which was far too small to be considered a city by my estimation. For safety I kept my passport and money with me while walking around the town at any time, a habit I kept for the whole of the trip.

One of my old workmates from Nhulunbuy was also staying here so we teamed up for a bit of exploring. Enjoying the time so much I stayed here for about 10 days and all for the princely sum of five dollars. The other occupants of the Hippie Hilton were two English guys, two Dutch girls and a Dutchman so we also became companions. The five of us were to cross paths on a few occasions later in the journey as we were all on our way to our home bases. My workmate from Nhulunbuy was just having a holiday on the cheap! This was certainly the place to do that.

The two girls and the two English guys and I decided to go to the far end of the island in Indonesian Timor to the town of Kupang, where there was an airport. After about a week we went

128

to the market place with the intention of getting on the bus to the airport. This 'bus' was once again a truck, and getting a seat on it was easier said than done. It filled up very quickly with people, cages with poultry in them and there just wasn't enough room on that day or the following two or three days. Eventually a local bloke came over and said if we were looking to get away from there he would be available to take us in his 4x4 wagon. The price he wanted was OK so the five of us arranged to meet him later that day.

We met him at the market place at 6 pm and climbed into the wagon which was pretty full, with the six of us and our backpacks. The route was nothing more than a dirt track after we left the town, and I was pretty sure after some time that this was not a main road between the capitals of East and West Timor. The man verified this and told us it was a short cut but this was the first time he had come this way. Well, that was a good time to tell us that when we were well on the way! This turned out to be a pretty eventful ride. The road that we should have taken was about seven hours travelling time. It actually took about 10 hours so that gives a good indication of the type of country we were taken through.

There were three significant events during the ride, all either exciting or frustrating. The first one came around midnight, when we got to a river. The driver stopped the wagon and told us he had to unload the weight to cross the river, then he had to find two white sticks on the other side which were the markers for the track to continue. After some negotiation he agreed to leave the backpacks and the Dutch girls and me on the river bank while the two English guys went with him to locate the sticks upriver. There was no way he was leaving all of us there for we were literally in the middle of what could only be described as a jungle. The noises we could hear after they left us were pretty unnerving as none of us had any idea what wildlife there was in Timor. It was almost a case of *Me Tarzan, You Jane* but I don't know how this Tarzan would

129

have fared against wild animals or crocodiles. I guess any of those could have been there. The weather was fine and it was a godsend that there was no rain. Finally, with some relief we saw headlights coming back downriver and the three of them in the wagon. They told us the two sticks were indeed upriver and the water was shallow enough for all of us to go together. The wagon was reloaded and the journey continued.

When we had left the river behind the driver informed us that there would be a village to pass through along the way. He said that when we got there the natives would rush to the wagon and follow us through the village and we were to have ready some small gifts to pass to them such as cigarettes or biscuits. Quite honestly I did not know what to expect or where he had brought us. My concerns escalated when he opened the glove box and took out a gun which he laid beside himself and told us that we must not stop the wagon while going through the village. The natives did indeed follow us through with many hands reaching out for the gifts we had managed to have ready to pass to them.

The third event came about at the end of the ride after we had been dropped off and the driver had been paid and left for his return to Dili. I am left wondering if he went back the same way as we had come, but I guess he might have taken the route he should have used in the first place!

We were dropped off at a beach around 5 am, and that day turned out to be very frustrating if not exciting. On the other side of the road opposite the beach was what looked like a fort. The driver had said that this was where we could get our passports attended to a bit later. After about an hour two or three soldiers came across and asked what we were doing here. When we explained where we had come from they left and came back with a vehicle and took us to a house in a small town. This turned out to be the Indonesian Consul and a man came to attend to us after the soldiers had spoken with him privately. The Consul official was not very happy because the driver had not taken us through the border post between East and West Timor. He had in fact smuggled us into Indonesia without us knowing. So we were made to wait until mid-afternoon before we were allowed to continue. We got our passports attended to and then found our way to the far end of the island and the airport at Kupang by bus. This time it was a regular bus even though a bit run down.

The airport here was very small but we were able to book a flight to our next stop Bali, for the next day. The aircraft turned out to be an old DC 10 which looked rather the worse for wear in my eyes but I presumed that it would have done many trips already so swallowed my concern and climbed aboard when the time came. Overnight was in a backpackers hostel in the city. So far on the trip backpackers seemed to be well catered for here on Timor.

Denpasar, Bali, INDONESIA

The flight turned out to be fine and as soon as we arrived at Bali's capital Denpasar I headed for Kuta Beach, the backpackers' haven. I had heard on the grapevine that the best accommodation choice on Bali was in small rooms which were built in the back yards of homes close to the beach. I found one which cost 50 cents a day so that suited me fine. The room was clean and comfortable with an endless supply of hot tea in a flask and a plate of cakes by the bedside. The bed was a regular single one and there was a toilet and a tub of cold water as well in a small room built on to the bedroom. The toilet was two foot holes to stand in and a hole in the floor to aim for. The tub was there to hold the water for bathing and flushing the toilet. No hot water but that was not needed. A ladle was used for bathing and flushing. Towels were also provided daily and all of this for 50 cents a day so I stayed for a few days in very comfortable surroundings.

I spent a lot of time at the beach and eating out at some of the cafés, and also used one of the many rickshaws and motorised tuk-tuks to get to the city, a few kilometres from Kuta Beach. These could also be hired to do a worthwhile tour for a couple of hours around the countryside. On another day at the beach I decided that even though I could not swim, there was no reason why I should stay out of the water, but after this I was much more careful whenever I went into the sea. I was only going to walk out to waist deep but when I was just about there the sand simply fell away in a steep drop. I had to scramble back to where I had been in a big hurry. That was pretty scary.

Magic mushrooms were available in a couple of the cafes but I was not going to get myself totally drugged,on those. There were others that did so and the outcome of that was enough to convince me not to try them out. I was having a pretty relaxing time here but I had to keep moving forward or stay here forever. I decided it was time to move on, keeping an eye on my budget for the move to Java.

There were two ways to get from Kuta Beach to Java, one was a flight from Denpasar and the other was overland and a short boat trip to follow. My thoughts are jumbled about this with both those options running around in my head; this jumble I am unable to fathom out. What I do know for sure is that I left Kuta Beach and then spent time at Djokjakarta on the neighbouring island of Java. I am left wondering if the magic mushrooms got into my food unawares to me while at Kuta Beach and messed around with my brain. There has to be a reason for being muddled on this passage. I guess cross contamination of food as well as practical jokes are not entirely unheard of!

Djokjakarta, Java, INDONESIA

I stayed for two or three days in the large city of Djokjakarta taking in the sights. Here I got to go close to a volcano near there as well. The villagers living close by it were taking huge risks by living there. There were temples to visit, cottage workshops making Batik wall hangings and clothing, and a very good shadow puppet show. I got around by bus mainly, most being pretty well maintained ones here when compared to the Timor buses. Those are etched in my memory all right. I spent a lot of time in the cafés here chatting with locals who were always eager for conversation. One topic that often got into these conversations was to be asked how it was living in Australia, especially by the younger ones.

I had been enjoying my time here; however, there was one small problem came about while travelling to Djakarta. I had caught up again with the Dutch girls and there was another Dutchman who joined our little group. I guess with all of us heading the same way it was a sure thing that our paths would keep on crossing, which was what kept happening later in the journey. I was OK with that as it was good to see familiar faces and chat about our experiences.

Anyway, back to the problem that occurred. The bus we caught for the first leg to Djakarta only went as far as a village along the way. There was not a connection there at the time but we were told a bus should be available at the next village about 20 kilometres away. It was mid-afternoon so after a chat amongst ourselves, with no transport we decided it would be OK to walk as it would be getting cooler towards the end of the day. We therefore did the walk with a short stop at a really small village we passed through on the way. The villagers said we must stop for a rest and made some tea for us to drink and chattered non-stop. We arrived at the next village and found out that the bus would not be going to

Djakarta until next day. So we spent the night at the village police station of all places as there were no accommodation places to stay at. We had been lucky to choose the police station for our enquiry about the bus because we were offered the station verandah out the back to stay on until next morning. Bathing facilities were the use of a small creek which flowed through the station garden.

We left on the bus next morning after thanking the police for their hospitality (which would not be so good in other circumstances I guess) and finally got to Djakarta. Here I decided a quick walk around the city centre was enough. Not the cleanest of cities by a long chalk. My next objective was to get to Singapore so with that in mind I sought out a travel agency to look at options. There was a ferry leaving the next day which I booked a passage on. How lucky was that!

The travel agent had not told me that the ferry did not go direct to Singapore, as I found out after boarding next day at the Djakarta docks. In fact it was a pretty big ship, with lots of passengers just lying about the decks. I was very glad I had splurged a bit on a cabin which was luxury compared to the deck. It was surprising to see that the galley kitchen was open to view. It was more surprising to see open flames from the cooking stoves in the kitchen, which made me a bit more than wary. But then when I read in a newspaper, sometime in the 80s I believe it was, that the ship had set on fire at sea and had been sunk then that did not surprise me one bit. Other than the ship being overfull the trip across to the island was enjoyable, as we passed quite a number of oil rigs on the journey. We went to a town on the Islands of Batam across the Straits towards Singapore, and changed to a small ferry boat, in rather dramatic style!

The ship dropped anchor about 300 metres from shore by my estimation. Passengers bound for Singapore were to disembark and would be taken the rest of the journey by another ferry boat.

Disembarking the ship was a joy to behold! A steel stairway had been lowered down the side of the ship to access a tender boat waiting to collect passengers at the foot of the stairway. The boat was what I would term a longboat, around six or seven metres long and about a metre wide. There were seats spaced across the boat less than one metre apart in single file. Probably eight passengers to each boat. There was an outboard motor at the stern and the stairway was positioned just in front of that. There were three problems to contend with, the stairway was fine but the sea had a pretty big swell which meant the distance from the bottom step to the boat was anything between two and eight feet. This of course meant the timing was critical. Added to this was the uncontrolled rocking and rolling of the boat as passengers made contact, some with an almighty thump. For the second time in Indonesia I was terrified being firstly a non-swimmer and secondly with a backpack of some 30 kilograms on my back and a shoulder bag with my safe-keeping stuff in it I would not be long in finding the sea bed if I was to fall into the water! When my turn came it was all or nothing so firstly passing my backpack to the boatman I just went for it when the boat came as close as it was going to at the bottom step. Thankfully I kept my balance and in fairness to the operator he was there to lend a hand, but very scary nonetheless.

A dozen passengers changed to the waiting ferry, a small cabin cruiser, at the quayside. Sailing into Singapore harbour was mind-boggling, and now I know why the harbour was named The Crossroads of the World years ago. There were so many ships I doubt I could have counted them in what was almost like a parking lot waiting to berth. That, of course, did not affect our ferry and I was real pleased to get on dry land again. Indonesia had given me a good insight into a new culture and all in all I had really enjoyed the trip through just a few of what are probably hundreds of islands that make up the country. In retrospect I guess my holding memories of Indonesia are a mixture of excitement, beautiful scenery and scary moments.

SINGAPORE

Customs at Singapore entry were very strict, hair especially came under their microscope, and any long hair amongst males had to be cut shorter. Mine was OK because it just grows outwards and not downward. I had been forewarned of this from travellers I had met along the way.

The two or three days I had planned to stay in Singapore stretched out to ten. The reason for that was my passport was due to expire in a few days' time, and it was best renewed in a city that had a British Embassy. After finding the embassy I was expecting to have a new one processed within two or three days, but this was not the case. After filling out the appropriate forms I was asked to come back in ten days, and there was no way I could get a change for the quicker out of the staff so I just had to accept the wait. I was instructed not to try to leave Singapore until my new passport had been authorised.

So it was ten days here on my budget, and the accommodation I found was on Racecourse Road which by the grapevine once again was where the budget accommodation was. It was better than I was expecting, clean and comfortable and not a bad place to hang out, quite close to the centre of the city and within walking distance to the waterfront and main areas. As I took to conserving my budget while waiting for my new passport I spent most days walking around the city taking in the sights and spending a lot of my meal breaks at Orchard Road or Chinatown with the many food stalls set up with lots of good cheap food to be had. Orchard Road had become one of my favourite places here.

Once again I splurged a bit on one of the days with a visit to Raffles Hotel. How could I come to Singapore again without making another visit to one of the world's most famous hotels? That was probably the only time I spent any cash on alcohol on the whole trip. Very enjoyable however, sitting in a tropical lounge with a nice cold beer or two. Also, I spent a lot of my evenings at the waterfront with the big stone lion fountain doing its routine. Here I found many locals and tourists spending time walking around or just sitting down in the cool of the evening. Many a conversation was struck up here, which was becoming a feature of the trip with lots of people just about everywhere I had been, eager to talk about themselves and also to listen to my tales about Australia.

I was relieved when the time came to go to the embassy to collect my passport. My next port of call was the railway station to book a trip up through Malaysia, my destination the city of Bangkok in Thailand. The train went direct to Bangkok with no changes to make and took the better part of a whole day to complete the journey. My memory recollects a rather old carriage with wooden seats and many other passengers to share my time with.

Bangkok, THAILAND

After arriving at the railway station I looked for information on where to find budget accommodation for a couple of days close to the city centre. The hotel I was directed to turned out to be very clean and right in the middle of the city. There was only one place that I wanted to see here and that was the Royal Palace which featured in the movie *The King and I* some time ago. So after a walk around during the evening and a good sleep I found my way to the river for a trip to the palace.

The river was wide and there were a lot of people there queuing for places on long boats to take them to the palace site. The boats were of the same type as the one which had collected me from the ferry on the high seas when leaving Java, with seating in single file for about eight people. As I made my way along the river's edge one of these boats pulled up alongside me and the boatman hailed me asking if I wanted to go to the palace. In retrospect I now know that I should have asked some questions before taking him up on his offer to take me there. He did take me which was fine and when we got there after a 15 minute trip, he asked how long I would be there so that he could be waiting for me to do the return trip. I told him I would stay for two hours and left it at that.

Two hours was just about enough time to take in the opulence of the palace, and going back to the river I found the boatman was sitting patiently in his dinghy, waiting for me. He saw me and hailed me again to get in for the return trip. There was no one else there for a ride but that was fine, at least until we got back to the starting point. The problem then was the river bank was some 20 metres from the boat and that is where he asked me for payment. That was the moment it dawned on me that I was being ripped off with the fare he asked for probably the cost of a whole boatload of people. When I complained about that he said it was either pay or swim, a real nice guy hey! Anyway discretion became the better part of valour, as my swimming capabilities were below zero. After some negotiation the money I gave him got me ashore but not the best result for me. Definitely ripped off!!

I spent the next day in the city and booked the next stage of the journey which was a flight to Calcutta in India for the following day. I was seated next to a young Thai woman on her way back to India to a city called Pune near Bombay and the university there. We had a real good chat during the flight and she said if I was to get to Bombay then why not make the trip to where she was living and she would be happy to meet me there and show me around the place. I was given an address of friends of hers who she said would make me welcome. Keeping the address just in case, I disembarked the flight at around 10 pm then set about finding my way to the centre of Calcutta.

Calcutta, INDIA

A bus from outside the airport was the cheapest way to get to the city centre. I found the one and only bus outside the terminal deserted and was totally surprised that there was nobody around to ask if I was at the correct place. Many times I had heard and read about the overcrowding to be expected in India, so to find the outside of the airport terminal totally deserted was way beyond my expectations. It seemed to me that waiting here was my best option until the driver of the bus at least turned up. I got onto the bus for a sit down, and it is still unfathomable to this day where they came from, but ten minutes had gone by when out of nowhere came the driver and a conductor. Quickly following on from that were more than a bus full of passengers all clamouring for seats. I stuck resolutely to my seat with my backpack firmly between my feet. In one minute flat I reckon the bus was filled to bursting point. The seat I had was a bench seat near the door and the conductor came for my fare. The thing to do now was to ask him to put me off near the main railway station, and thankfully he agreed. How he got around the bus to collect his fares I have no idea but he either did or else gave up because he was back in just a few minutes. An Indian guy who sat beside me said he would tell me when I was near the station. The time came when he said that I should get off the bus but I should have waited for the conductor to tell me because it was the wrong railway station.

The station was directly across a busy road crowded with traffic and people. I made my way across to the ticket office and told the attendant that I wished to get a train to Bombay. He told me that this was not the main line station, but it was about a mile along the road. At least it seemed that I was on the right track anyway. I walked there and found out that a ticket across India to Bombay with the option of taking time off the train at any place along the journey was available here. The thing that had to be decided was a place to sleep and the station seemed to fit the bill. I had never expected to see so many of the populace sleeping at the station. There were whole families there cooking and sleeping. My last food had been on the flight to Calcutta so I had no choice but to eat whatever I could find without getting Delhi Belly. There was food at a stall nearby which had bread and egg so I figured that there should be no problem with either of those. While in India I was to keep off meat if I could. After that supper I settled down for my first sleep out at a railway station which at least was warm and dry.

Bathing facilities at the station were very limited with only a small sink with a cold water tap in the toilets. With this my only option I had to make do. That was the washing facilities for several days from here on; not many more real beds and bathing until getting to London. A few but not many. After my wash I went to the ticket office and bought a ticket to Bombay for the next day, with plans to spend that day in Calcutta. It was correct that I could get on and off the train at will, so figuring that the Ganges River was the only place I really wanted to see along the route at Benares it was my plan to have a couple of days there on the way across India.

The day in Calcutta was spent wandering around within walking distance of the station taking in the culture of the city. Some memorable moments are the incredible number of people begging for handouts and the biggest outdoor laundry imaginable with probably at least a hundred women, all in their own small space in their white shawls bashing and wringing clothes in water coming from somewhere. Spring or piped water I could not work out, the
140

area was about the size of a football field with large stones for the bashing of the clothes on. Passing by two or three times during the day it was always packed with women.

It was not unusual to see sick people lying around on the street and I was starting to realise the poverty of India. This was not so widespread in later years, but right here right now the poverty was definitely evident. After the day's walking I returned to my current abode for a sleep before catching the train next morning.

After my wash and a breakfast of more bread and omelette I ventured onto the station platform to wait for the train. Very soon the platform filled to capacity I would not hesitate to say, and I was thankful that I had a front row spot. The crowd stretched the whole length of the platform, three or four people deep. When I saw a train reversing along the line to the waiting throng I prepared myself for a dash to the nearest door when it came to a stop. It was too late for that to make a difference, as the train carriages were already pretty well filled with people who must have wandered down the line to the train while it was parked there. The stories I had heard from passing travellers were fast becoming a reality - it is the quick ones that get the seats. I did manage to get on the train and parked myself in a corner of a carriage sitting on my backpack.

The carriage was filled to capacity when a whistle blew at the other end of it. There was a centre aisle between the seats and a soldier with a baton braced across his chest started to herd the people down the aisle and off the train at the opposite end of the carriage while bellowing out that this was a military carriage. The people being herded out were wailing and carrying on about the situation but moving off the train just the same. By the time he got to me sitting in the corner the carriage was empty other than about 10 or a dozen soldiers who had followed the baton guy onto the train. He stopped and looked at me sitting on my backpack and very quietly said that this was a military carriage. My reply somewhat sheepishly was that I needed to get to Bombay and before I could say anything more his reaction was instantaneous when he asked if I was English. When I told him, Yes I was, he then said, "Then take a seat, sir!!" The soldiers were only on the train for no more than 15 minutes before they got off so there I was with a whole carriage to myself.

That was only brief however, as the train was soon to get more people on at other stops. I believe I must have been on a regular train rather than an express because the train stopped many times with the result being a very crowded carriage in a pretty short time. This caused me to have a change of plan. The plan had been to go to Benares (which is now Varanasi) and the Ganges River on the train but with all the people now on board I was very uncomfortable, so at the next stop I decided to get off and catch a train to continue the ride later. Later proved to be the next day as that was when the next train would be stopping at this station.

It was only a small town where I was and outside the station was a group of young men who were, of all things, playing marbles on the ground. *What a strange thing for young men to be doing,* I thought, and they were obviously taking things very seriously with all the agitation going on. It brought back schoolyard memories for me. It was with discretion that I kept my distance anyway as I did not wish to get embroiled in a game of marbles. My time was spent in a small café for most of the afternoon and at the end of the day I finished up sleeping at the station after strolling around the town for the rest of the time. The train next day took me to Benares where I found a budget hotel and stayed for two days taking in the daily life of the city.

Benares (Now Varanasi), INDIA

I found the city just as over-populated as Calcutta. The two days here were spent soaking up the culture with throngs of people bathing in the River Ganges. I had learned that the Hindus travel great distances to do this, for the religious significance. The amount of temples to various gods of faith was another memorable sight. The begging for handouts here was on a par with Calcutta and the temples seemed to be a popular place for this activity. It was not easy to keep from handing out some money to them but I had a journey to finish on my budget so really had no alternative other than not to give.

I had read of the dead being cremated on the banks of the river and though I saw none where I was, smoke was rising on the banks in the distance, so I presumed that was what was happening there. I had no desire to witness the funerals and would have been a bit rude I think to do so anyway. It had been two more days of extreme culture shock when I boarded the train again after my time here and settled down for another crushed ride.

It was a nice surprise this time as it was not so crowded as the previous rides. On this train I shared a seat with a young chap who was on his way home from the university at Hyderabad. His home was at a hill station where his father was in the army. We got along pretty well and he suggested that I break my journey at his stop and take a look at the hill station while I had the opportunity. That seemed to be a good idea as I had read of these places so decided to do just that. We got off the train where there was a connecting train after a short waiting time. The ride was for about an hour and climbed steadily through some lush vegetation as we got higher to the hill station. His father was waiting for him in his army uniform and after having some time talking with them they left me to have a look around the place. It was pretty small and much cooler than where we had left from, very pleasant really and a world away from the three places I had already visited. Very few people and no sign of anyone begging or sick. The train, an old steam locomotive, was there for an hour before making its way back to the station some way below us. The line was a spur line so travelled no further. When the train was ready to leave I got back on to it after deciding that the look around I had was enough and could see no point in staying here overnight. The railway station below was where I slept in the waiting room; bathing once again was a cold water tap.

My day there was spent wandering around the area near the station, waiting until the train to Bombay arrived. I bought some pears from a street trader and took them back to the railway station to eat while waiting for the train. There were three young boys playing around there and when I started to eat my fruit they came over to where I was sitting with a hungry look in their eyes.

As I sliced the fruit I passed pieces to them to eat, and the marble-topped table at which I was sat became wet from juice which had dropped onto it while slicing. As this was attracting flies I picked up a piece of rag which was on the table and wiped the table dry with it. For some reason one of the boys started to cry and when I asked what the matter was one of his friends told me that I had just used his shirt to wipe off the juice from the table. Well just how bad did that make me feel? I told the boy I was sorry and opened my rucksack and gave him one of my tee shirts. Probably much too big for him but the pleasure that replaced the tears was gold!

My eating habits for the past few days had been foods from either a shell or with the skin on, eggs, bread and fruit mainly. My senses had me very aware of contaminated food in India being common and that was also the case with water. With this in mind I was keeping from drinking any water other than boiled. This is where the railways of the country helped because at every stop the train made there would be hawkers selling tea by passing a small cup of the beverage through the open carriage windows for a very small price. The hawkers would have a very large kettle of tea and serve it in small clay cups much the same shape as a miniature plant pot. Might be a bigger business producing them than what selling the tea is with no returning of the cups seeming to happen.

Bombay (Now Mumbai), INDIA

The train to Bombay arrived and I was once more on my way forward. It was a two-day planned stay before continuing on to Agra to visit the Taj Mahal. Leaving the Bombay station I booked into a budget hotel for a couple of nights and took to exploring around the city. It was good to find showers and toilets here for a long-awaited good clean up of myself. The situation here was much the same as the other two large cities I had visited regarding the begging especially. When the two days had elapsed I remembered the offer that I had got from the Thai student on the flight from Calcutta. With that I figured *Why not go there?* before moving on so I made a decision to book a ticket on the train to Pune and set off on a bit of a side-track to my plans. The train to Pune was similar to the one to the hill station and was climbing for much of the way for about an hour. Once there at the terminus I set out to find the address that the Thai student had given me.

Pune, INDIA

It did not take long to find the address which was on a quiet road, a detached house with a large garden. The young guy who

145

came to answer my knocking was a local who let his rooms out to uni students and when I explained why I was there he already was expecting me to call at sometime. It is with regret that I cannot recall the name of the girl who gave me the address but it unfortunately escapes me. I know it was a real tongue twister as lots of Thai names can be. Anyway, the young guy asked how long I would be staying for and as I told him that it would be no more than a few days he let me have a room for free. How nice was that! There were a couple of other young Indian guys there as well and all became pretty friendly to get along with. I ended up staying for three or four days.

After the introductions to all of them at the house, one of them took me to the university to catch up with the Thai student. Upon finding her she invited the two of us to a meal where she stayed with three other girlfriends and that was to be my evenings for the whole time I was there. Dinner Thai-style with home cooking by the girls. No table or chairs but a blanket on the floor with cushions and all manner of food laid out to choose from. My no-meat philosophy went out of the window for those meals with them all being delicious and no upset belly at all. The days were spent in the town when there was free time from the uni and it was here that I saw my one and only Bollywood movie at a local cinema, a weird and wonderful movie that was, deadly serious then breaking out into song and dance for no reason at all.

All in all the Thai and Indian hospitality here had been first class but the time came when I must keep moving. It would have been easy to stay there as it was such a nice city to be in but I was on my way back to family and friends after all. At the railway station I was sent off by the girl who had invited me, and one of her friends also came so goodbyes were said after having had a real nice time at Pune. It was then off back to Bombay to get the train going to Agra and the Taj Mahal.

Agra

Arriving at Agra on the train from Bombay found me outside the railway station spoilt for choice for some transport to the Taj Mahal site. There were any number of taxis, tuk-tuks and cycle rickshaws. It was a rickshaw I chose after finding out that it was the cheapest price for the ride. It took about ten minutes to make the trip and off I went to see the building that I had seen glimpses of while on the rickshaw. Wow! What a sight to take the breath away when viewed as you enter the water garden that leads the eyes towards the building. It was even more outstanding the closer I got to it and I was just awestruck so many times over the next couple of hours or so. The beauty of the memorial is pretty well impossible to put into words and really needs to be seen to understand that statement. Twenty-two years in the making by a man for the love of his wife, mind-blowing stuff. Up above the entry arches there are 22 bells spaced out to signify this fact. After having walked around the site for a while I sat down just to take it all in as this was most likely the only time I would be here. A girl was sitting close by looking just as awestruck as I was and when we got chatting that was one thing that we had in common, we both agreed it was the most beautiful thing to be seeing. I stayed at another backpackers' hotel after a busy day and headed to Jaipur on a train the next day.

Jaipur

Jaipur is known as the Pink City, as the old city buildings are nearly all built with a stone pink in colour. Here I spent two days once again in backpackers' accommodation. Much of one day was spent at an old site which was an observatory for looking at the solar system. There was a lot of ancient equipment here which was or had been used for tracking the planets etc. There was not, as far as I could see, any indication of any of it being used at the time, with no other person at the site but me. The equipment would be far outdated by now.

There were a large number of big monkeys on free range about the city especially in residential areas but they did not cause me any concern. Being residential I guess there were plenty of food scraps around the houses to keep them occupied. It was very hot and dusty here so I did not linger for very long on my walking and bought myself a black umbrella to use as a sunshade. These were not uncommon to see here and it got a fair bit of use over the next week or two. From Jaipur I took the train once again, this time to New Delhi.

New Delhi

When I was on my way back to Australia in 1970 on the bus tour that came to grief in Afghanistan, it was at New Delhi where that overland trip ended. I then had a flight to Darwin to return to Australia. So it was here in the city of New Delhi that I had planned to fly directly to England having done what I had set out from Darwin to do over two months earlier. It was here that I also changed that plan. I was enjoying the trip so much that I thought *Why not keep going?* I checked my budget and decided that seeing as I had forwarded some money to my bank's branch in London then if I was running my budget down too much I should be able to access that if needed. With that in mind I stayed for two nights and took in some of the culture of life here, pretty much the same as the other big city Bombay. One thing I did was to go for a look around the Red Fort which was a good thing and worth the visit.

It was so hot here I actually thought I would treat myself to a beer or two and went into a large hotel only to find it was so expensive that I did not bother to follow up on that. With budgeting I had become very conscious how my money was spent. For the night time I was sleeping again at the railway station here and the first night had a bit of excitement. After I had settled down to a slumber I felt some movement on my face. I came to with a start and found that an Indian bloke had been trying to remove my spectacles from my face! He let go of them as he took flight so I was lucky not to have them stolen. A railway policeman must have seen it happen because he came over to me and told me to have a sleep on a long flat trolley which was just by his office and that he would keep an eye on me until morning. Thankfully, I slept well that night under guard. If that had been in a western society then no doubt I would have been given marching orders out of the railway station, but not in India.

The route I planned would pretty much follow the way I had previously travelled in reverse so that meant a train to Peshawar in Pakistan for starters. After making a booking for the train I then boarded the one to take me there via Amritsar with a connecting train from there. I arrived at Peshawar and booked into the same hostel that I had used the last time here.

Peshawar, PAKISTAN

This was a bustling city with crowds of people thronging the main part where I was. One morning was almost taken up at a bank when changing some travellers' cheques and the process was laboured and slow. This was my first time of having an extended

149

delay at a bank for this purpose on the trip. It was here that I figured it was time I got my hair cut as it was rather bushy by now and as I had not shaved since leaving Darwin my face was also sporting a fair bit of hair growth. Upon seeing a barber's pole on a side street I ventured in there to have a clean-up. I sat down in the shop which had an earthen floor and seeing the half dozen or so locals waiting I figured that I was mixing with the tribesmen that we were warned about on my previous trip to these parts. I felt brave enough to wait my turn, but changed my plan a little and decided just to have a trim and forgot about removing the beard I had grown. This cemented itself when I saw the barber sharpening the cut throat razor for another guy in a chair. Discretion became the better part of valour for not the first time travelling. Everything went fine however, and I think my fears were unwarranted. My beard remained in place however!

A small group of backpackers came to the hostel and while we were chatting I mentioned that my next stop was Kabul in Afghanistan. However, they informed me that the border was closed. There had been some political turmoil there in the country and that was the reason. Of course I believed them but I figured it would not hurt to go and check it out myself rather than just backtrack to another route. So I boarded the bus and after a dusty ride through the Khyber Pass it reached the border with Afghanistan. When I went to the passport control table on the Pakistani side the officer there told me the same as I had heard before leaving. The border was closed to foot travellers but was open for anyone in a vehicle to pass through into Afghanistan. I in my wisdom argued that I could see a bus parked over the Afghan side and I would like to try and use that as a vehicle. The officer stamped my passport out of Pakistan telling me I was wasting my time. Walking across the strip of land to the Afghan border about 70 or 80 metres I gathered my wits together for some negotiating.

150

There were a couple of soldiers at the border, and one of them asked me what I wanted. My request was to use the bus to continue on across the country, only to be met with blunt refusal. I persisted until things got a little serious. When I saw the soldier taking his rifle from his shoulder and using it in what I saw as a threatening manner, discretion again took over in my thinking over the situation. It was a hasty retreat that I made back to the Pakistani border. There was a smile on the face of the officer there when he stamped my passport back into the country. Luckily for me the bus was still there so I got a return trip through the Khyber Pass and back to Peshawar.

Back at the city I needed to work out an alternative route, as I was not going to just cave in and head back to London by air. I needed to find a way to skirt around Afghanistan. I found out that there was a border with Iran to the south of Pakistan, and that the railway had a route to get me there. It meant first to get to a town called Quetta to the south, where the Iranian Consulate could provide a visa to enter Iran. So it was a train which took me to the east and the south, then west to Quetta on the way to Iran.

Quetta

Arriving at Quetta I found the Consulate for Iran, a house in its own grounds with only one man there as far as I could make out. He turned out to be the officer, in the process of moving his furniture around in the house. When I told him that I wanted a visa to enter Iran he said that will be fine but would I mind helping him with the moving of his furniture first? About an hour later we got around to dealing with my request. A most unusual visa application to say the least! It was another night of sleeping at a railway station at Quetta. Good job there were waiting rooms for this and toilets with running water for bathing of sorts.

To travel into Iran meant another train ride to a town called Zahedan which was some distance across the Pakistan/Iran border. This train just had to be the slowest on Earth, I would think. The reason given was the poor state of the track. It was so slow that some people got off now and again to walk alongside of it. A person's walking speed I believe is six kilometres an hour and if that is a fact then that was the speed of the train through some very arid regions of the planet. I felt that this train ride would be endless. It actually went for about 750 kilometres from Quetta and needless to say, I lost all track of time while on the train.

At Quetta railway station I had come upon a trio of two girls and a bloke. They were also doing the same thing as I was and finding the alternative route into Iran. When the train finally got to its destination I discovered that the two English guys who had been with me at Timor had been on the train also and so the group of us booked into a hotel at Zahedan.

Zahedan, IRAN

The hotel we found had some beds made up in the forecourt outside. At reception we were told that they were the budget accommodation, ridiculously cheap, so we all took the offer for the night to come. I figured that if the beds were made up outside then the chance of rain must be close to zero. It was about midday at the time, so dropping our backpacks after assurances that they would be safe left on the beds, we split up for looking around the place. It was pretty hot with the sun just about at baking point. Later that afternoon all the guys had returned to the hotel when the two girls came back accompanied by three local boys, and after a chat it was decided that we would all meet for a meal at a restaurant recommended by the three boys. After making those arrangements they left us until later. The restaurant did prove to

152

be a good one and I was not at all dubious about eating a meat dish here, it was the salad that came with it that I was a bit wary of. I still reckon that I was eating grass! During the meal the boys explained where to catch a bus to continue onward.

The next day we boarded the bus and it got really full with passengers and baggage. What was strange was the large number of sacks and pillow cases being brought on board and stowed in just about every available space, including racks above the seats as well as spaces below. Some passengers were actually cradling some on their laps. The bus eventually got away and after a short distance of about five kilometres, after going around a roundabout at the edge of town the bus stopped and two uniformed men got on board. Pandemonium broke out. The reason for that was the locals on board were asked to remove the bags from the bus. So the bus was turned around to go back into town to do that, at least that is what I thought was being done. Instead of that the bus got to the roundabout again and just did a full circle around it to return once again to the men who had boarded about ten minutes ago. We had a repeat performance there and were turned around again.

Of course I began to wonder just what was in the bags, thinking it was probably drugs. Anyway the trip back to town gave us another repeat performance at the roundabout with once again a full circle and another trip back to the uniformed men. They once again boarded and another repeat performance was about to be carried out when one of the guys from the hotel lost his cool and demanded that the bags be removed here and now, so that we could get on with the journey. With that the uniformed men took a few of the bags and sent us on our way. The contents of the bags turned out to be not drugs, but would you believe it, tea! That commodity must have a good market in Iran, I guess.

My next objective was to get to the city of Tehran, the capital of Iran and with about 1500 kilometres to travel on buses I settled down to the task. It turned out that I was to have the company of the other five travellers from here to Tehran so it was good to have that, as the landscape did not offer much for interest as it was so arid. Often I compared this to the areas of Australia when I was in similar conditions but I was to recall the beauty of the sunsets and sunrises and the vibrant colours generated by them. This is not to mention the night sky in such places as the Pilbara of Western Australia or Arnhem Land in the Northern Territory. There had also been the night sleeping under the stars of the Milky Way in western Queensland, miles from any artificial light which was just magic. Looking through the windows of the buses I travelled on I found the countryside of Iran to be largely devoid of vegetation. Much of it was the sandy and stony desert which seems to abound in this part of the world; there was not the beauty of the Australian outback as I remembered it. The highway we travelled on across the country went pretty much diagonally from Zahedan to Tehran with a couple of bus changes on the way.

Tehran, IRAN

Arriving at Tehran I spent a few days at the same hotel that I had stayed at on the opposite journey some two years previously. I used the time for just relaxing ready for the next hop across Turkey. This again was done using buses in the same way as I had on the rides across Iran. Now I was starting to keep an even sharper eye on my finances at hand with about another 2000 kilometres to travel on to Istanbul and then probably another 3000 to London. I had been pretty frugal with my spending so far but even more of a tight belt from here on would be needed as funds were getting a bit on the low side. There was still my back up cash in London but the main reason for having that there was so that if or when I wished to return to Australia again then I had a fare ready and waiting for me. That had been my strategy on my two previous trips back to England

Continuing on towards Turkey with a hop on and hop off buses plan of attack, there always seemed to be a connection for onward travel at the changeover stops along the way so I was confident in that regard. The journey took me two or three days to complete this way across Iran and at one stop I even sold my trusty umbrella which I had bought in India as a sunshade, to a man just sitting and taking things easy in the sunshine, for the price of the next bus fare.

Istanbul, TURKEY

It was good to finally arrive at Istanbul in Turkey, feeling rather weary. Here I had booked a budget hostel for a day or two to have some more exploring around the city as it was most unlikely I would be here again in the future. My arrival at Istanbul had seen our little group of travellers from Iran dwindle in number to just me, solo again.

I retraced my steps to the mosques and the bazaar, a place to spend hours if inclined to. There was so much going on here in the city with all kinds of cottage industries for want of a better description apart from the hundreds of stalls selling wares in the bazaar. There were silversmiths, goldsmiths and jewellery makers to name a few, displaying their skills as well as selling the fruits of their work.

After getting myself refreshed and ready for the next part of my journey I booked a train ticket to Munich in Germany. This trip covered about 2000 kilometres and passed through Bulgaria, then Yugoslavia and on through Austria before getting to Munich.

Munich, GERMANY

At Munich I realised that I was now down to a very low level in my budget after finding my way to the same camping ground that I had enjoyed so much when last at Munich. How I got there I have no idea right now but with only a small amount of cash with me it sure would not have been a taxi!

My luck was in however, because I ran into one of the English blokes who I had travelled with on some parts of the journey, the last time having been on the buses across Iran. He was now solo and had a tent there so I got to sleep under canvas that night instead of under the stars as I had intended. The next day we set out together for the autobahn to get thumbing lifts for either Belgium or France to get a ferry across the English Channel. He had first luck with a small car stopping for him and that was the last time I saw him.

It was not long before I got a lift in a car and was dropped off outside Frankfurt. There I had to decide to either go into the city or just keep on trying to move forward. It was late afternoon by now and the city of Frankfurt skyline was far into the distance. That made my decision for me to keep going forward and it proved to be a lucky choice. A truck driver stopped for me and he turned out to be going onward to Calais in France which was where the Channel Ferry to Dover in England left from. He dropped me right at the gate next morning and that was after he let me have a snooze on his bed behind the seats while he drove through the night. On top of that he paid for a breakfast for me next morning at a roadside tavern, after I had told him that I had

156

not enough cash on me to afford one. What a legend that Belgian guy was!

After I bought a ferry ticket I was left with the princely sum of less than one pound after a currency conversion. That was the amount of money I landed with at Dover. I had set out from Darwin just about 4 months earlier with 750 Aussie dollars in travellers' cheques and a flight ticket to Timor so I do believe I had got value for money along with having had a terrific holiday on this trip.

Dover, ENGLAND

So here I was back in my home country with not very much in cash, but money to look forward to after getting to London. My next objective however, was my home at Shaw so I went to the railway station at Dover and asked if it would be possible to have my brother phoned to ask if he could pay for a ticket for me to get to Manchester, and pay for my ticket that way. The bloke at the ticket office looked at me and asked me what I thought the railway system was, did I think it just did things on a whim? Needless to say he knocked me back on the request. I then had the thought, yes that is one reason why the Aussies call us Pommie bastards. A bit of flexibility would have been appreciated. There was no alternative other than to hit the road with my thumb. A car with a young couple in it stopped for me and asked where I was heading. I told them I wanted to get into London but they only went part of the way. I told them how much I had and asked if that would be enough for a train fare from where they could take me. They said yes that would be enough, and it was with three shillings that I arrived in London.

London

In the centre of London I went to my Australian bank's branch with my passbook to withdraw some money to continue on my way home.

"Too late!" was the cry from the teller. At 3.05 in the afternoon it was five minutes after the bank had closed for business for the day. Oh well, that meant one more night sleeping rough so where else but another railway station? I ended up at Waterloo Station. Spending my last cash on a sandwich and then drinking some water at the station I settled down for a long wait for the next morning. Thankfully, I was not moved on. Next day I was at the bank bright and early to withdraw some cash, and with money in my wallet I ventured to Euston Station where the trains to Manchester departed from. I spotted what was named a Super Loo there, and after entering I realised that in here one could shower, have a haircut and shave and generally get cleaned up. So rather than go to my parents' house in my state which was very untidy to say the least, with a large growth of hair and beard, about an hour or so later I was transformed into a more respectable person with a goatee beard and much thinner hair. My clothes were not too bad so I kept to them until I was back at Shaw.

I got onto a train and was in Manchester by the afternoon. From the station I took a bus which passed by the road into Shaw where another bus would complete the journey. I was unlucky enough to see the back of that bus having just missed a connection. My parents' house was now about three kilometres away so I decided to walk the final piece of my journey. I can honestly say that the walk was a piece of cake to do with no effort needed at all. While I was in the Super Loo at Euston Station I had weighed myself and tipped the scales at nine and a half stones. I know that prior to leaving Darwin in the Northern Territory those four months earlier I had been over the weight of thirteen stones. That knowledge left me feeling very fit and that was the case right then. I had phoned home from London at the railway station so it was soon after a welcome home that my mother had a hot meal for me on the dining table which was most enjoyable. I was happy to be back at Shaw spending the next few days catching up with family and old friends.

Shaw

So here I was back in Shaw again with the same decision to make that had to be made last time I was here. To stay or not to stay? It was definite that I would not just turn around but I would take some time to consider what the outcome would be. It was not very long before I approached my two old workmates who I had worked for on another time here, and once again asked for work for an unknown amount of time. They were fine about that and I was given a job with them.

I was enjoying time with my old friends, and now that Christmas was not so far off I decided I would stay until then before thinking of any move to another horizon. During this time I was watching some TV at the house and the programme was the telecast of the opening of the Sydney Opera House at Sydney Harbour so I was happy to see some of my old places of leisure. It was there on the opposite side foreshore that I would spend a fair bit of time just lying on the grassed areas planning moves or just taking in the nice weather for a while. The area there was one of my favourite spots.

One evening at the house there was a knock at the door and it was one of my work mates. A hotel having Christmas functions while working around renovations had a loss of power, and he was asking if I was free to go to check it out. It was around 6 pm and a bitterly cold and snowbound evening. Going to the hotel I found a problem with a back-up generator. The town areas were on a roster for power supply at this time due to coal shortages for the power stations. The hotel had its own back-up generator in use that day because of the roster system. The generator was in a small enclosure outside and so cold with my hands just about freezing up doing the work. It was here that I decided a return to Australia was imminent! It was in the New Year that I started the ball rolling in that regard.

There had been a couple of occasions since arriving back in Shaw that I had been sick for a couple of days. On the last occasion I figured it best if I consulted a doctor who happened to be a Pakistani doctor. I told him I had been travelling through his part of the world and he immediately diagnosed me with malaria. When I told him that I would be returning to Australia in the near future his advice was to ride it out until then, and to get to a hospital while the sickness was evident. He prescribed some medication which he said could help but with so many strains of malaria that was uncertain. He said an Australian hospital would be a better option than a local one, Heaven knows why. However, I did as he said and yes, the hospital in Sydney when the sickness returned did fix me up with no recurrence to this day.

1974

Early in the New Year I made my move to return to Australia. My mate who had travelled with me previously was now living in Shaw again, and was also keen to return to Australia so we booked flights to Sydney from London. We travelled to London and got into a spot of bother at Heathrow airport preparing for our departure, somehow or other we got confused with our gate number and lined up for a flight to the USA, and had to be redirected to the correct one for Sydney. Just a little more than embarrassing, luckily our flight was for a later time.

Sydney, AUSTRALIA

At Sydney we were met by some of our good mates and then taken to the communal house of theirs at Neutral Bay on the North Shore of the harbour. This house had become a haven for our group of mates over the years. However, there was not enough room for the two of us as well as the guys already there. So we took a short lease on a flat in North Sydney not very far from Neutral Bay near our mates' house. We were soon joined at our flat by another mate from Shaw who was in Australia doing some travelling himself.

The first port of call in the city was the multi-storey building that I had worked on for the time spanning the end of 1972 and the new year of 1973 which was now in its final stages of completion. It was work that I was looking for and the company rehired me. I began working with the same foreman as before and after a couple of weeks there was a site visit from our boss at head office, to see me. There was quite a surprise to come when he gave me a proposition that I take on the foreman's position on the electrical work on the rebuilding of a major hotel in the city along with a new multi-storey building which would house it. Accepting the job I moved onto the site which was only a couple of blocks away from the site that I was working on. It was close to Circular Quay and was about to be started after the demolition work on the old hotel had been done. Very soon however, I had a change of heart about the job as I began to realise that the time I would be here would be two years or so and did not feel a bit ready to be that settled just yet. That thought led me to explain myself to my boss and he understood my feelings so I moved on.

Soon I was checking the job adverts in the Sydney Morning Herald to find that a hotel in Sydney was looking for electricians. It was good to spend some time living and working in Sydney with many good weekends spent on the night life of the city. There was also a weekend or two spent further afield.

One of them was a long weekend trip to Forster on the Central Coast of NSW. Forster was an up and coming tourist town with many homes being built there and a small RSL club near a camping ground. It was necessary to remind myself to be on my best behaviour when we went there for a few beers and a meal. No repeats of Adelong, with that 9 pm fiasco still in the forefront of my mind. From memory there were five of us who went for the weekend break.

There was one mishap with our hired large ex-army tent which did not have a floor to it and no groundsheet either. We put it up after arriving in town and finding the camping ground. After that we left it to go for the rest of the day and night's entertainment, then it was back to the tent and into sleeping bags. When we awoke next morning the first to leave the tent got into trouble on his way out. Unknown to us we had put the tent up where a colony of bull ants also camped and he unwittingly trod on their place of rest to send them scattering. The poor bloke got a huge bite on his foot and that was obviously very painful. He hopped around like some demented person and the rest of us were very careful trying not to have the same misfortune.

Another weekend I had a solo bus trip to the ski fields in the Snowy Mountains of NSW. I had been skiing at Thredbo in earlier times and had got to a reasonable standard then so I was itching for another go. It was a Friday bus trip, to return on the Sunday afternoon so a good bit of time for skiing. Accommodation was dormitory style so plenty of others to mix with for the weekend. It was a worthwhile trip but not long enough to go often.

Sydney was proving to be a lot of fun and I continued working at the hotel for a while longer before the time came when I figured it was time to move on for some more country work. I saw an advert for electricians once again in the Sydney Morning Herald to work on a power station being built at a town called Wallerawang which was about two hours' drive from Sydney across the Blue Mountains. After getting a job it was off to Wallerawang by train from Sydney.

Wallerawang, NSW

When the train was entering the small town of Wallerawang there was a light dusting of snow on the ground, and I wondered whether or not I had done the right thing by coming here if it was a cold place to work. However, it was just about the end of winter, and it did turn out to be a mild climate. The days got pretty warm soon especially with all the stairs to climb up and down on the job. This was the third stage of the power station here with the first two stages already up and running. The first month I was here I went back to Sydney on the train to have my weekends there, not my usual way of being on country work but with only an hour and a half to Sydney and no night life as such, just one pub and nothing else the temptation was too much to let go by.

By now I had purchased a car, another Morris Mini. This would have been my fifth time of owning a Mini. My two Shaw mates had decided on one of my visits to Sydney to go back to Waller-awang with me to check the town out. They wound up getting jobs on the power station, staying at the pub for accommodation. Mine was in the construction camp cabins so maybe none were available for them. One of them actually ended up working with me to lay and tie cables on the cable trays which were in place around the construction. This went on for a couple of months up until the Christmas break when we returned to the house at Neutral Bay to the guys who lived there. After Christmas I did not return to Wallerawang but instead I got a job advertised again in the Sydney Morning Herald which was at a town called Narrabri in northern NSW. The New Year saw me start work there.

1975

Narrabri, NSW

Leaving Sydney in my car I picked up another electrician at Parramatta west of Sydney to take with me to Narrabri for starting work there. We drove there, arriving in the mid afternoon with instructions to find a house there which served the purpose of both office and accommodation. After finding the house we were directed to a local school to be set to work right away. The accommodation was a caravan set up in the garden of the house and a brick toilet and shower block had been erected there also for use. Most of the work was at the local schools during their summer holiday and some work around the town and surrounding area after the schools had returned to lessons.

One particular job was at a farming property about an hour's drive out of town to do a minor repair within the homestead, about an hour's work. The work actually lasted for the better part of two days there with all the extra work that was done after the repair job. The lady owner made full use of my being there to get all the little electrical jobs done that had been piling up.

There were three of us electricians living in the caravan and there was one night which had a humorous ending. What led up to it was a tree which was situated right next to the caravan. There was also an annexe to the van with three camp beds in it. It had been my choice to elect to use one of these for sleeping, a bit cooler than inside the caravan. Blankets were not needed so I would just sleep in a sleeping bag on the bed and would leave that lying on the bed during the day. It was unknown to me why I had suddenly developed a very itchy rash in my groin. When I say very itchy that is exactly what I mean. It was not until I told one of the local electricians of the problem while out for a few beers one night that I found out a caterpillar which the locals call itchy grubs had got into my sleeping bag causing the problem. He told me the grubs loved to eat leaves of the cedar tree next to the caravan and would have found their way into the bag from there.

Later that night, after having checked my bag for itchy grubs it must have played on my mind because upon waking at about 2 am I woke the other two guys in the van when they found me attempting to cut down the cedar tree with my hacksaw. I only managed to get half way through the trunk so I did not get the job finished. The grubs however, must have taken flight as the problem went away from then on. That is, the immediate problem did because for a number of years thereafter the rash reappeared every year for about three months at the same time as the problem had started. Thankfully it gradually went away but was evident for a number of years to come.

A lot of my time here was spent working on the large water pumps that provided irrigation to the huge cotton growing paddocks which abound around the Narrabri area from the Namoi River. There was also a fair bit of work at the town's flour mill and at the schools of course. Night life was the pubs and the RSL club so that was mostly restricted to the weekends. I stayed here until midyear and then returned to Sydney to be best man for my mate from the Exmouth days and beyond at his wedding.

Sydney

I did not return to Narrabri but found myself a job in North Sydney on a new multi-storey building which was being constructed. When I had been there for a few days, who should I see on site but my old boss from the job at Nhulunbuy in the Northern Territory. We had a night out shortly after with some good chatting as we caught up on old times.

During this time another trip to New Zealand eventuated. I had resumed living at the house at Neutral Bay with my friends, and three of us decided on a holiday to New Zealand to do some skiing. We booked flights to Christchurch on the South Island for skiing at Mt Hutt out of Christchurch for one week and Coronet Peak near Queenstown for another week.

Christchurch, NEW ZEALAND

At the airport we were met by the driver of a mini bus and taken to Methven, the small country town at the foot of the mountain range where Mt Hutt was situated. We were taken to the one pub in town, our home for the next six days. It was clean and comfortable accommodation with bed and breakfast the deal, and there was the mini bus to take us up the mountain daily. The bus came for us after breakfast and took us to the slopes for our day of skiing. There was a ridge to cross on the way which was very narrow and we were told by our driver that if the wind was fierce then it would be unsafe to cross the ridge. Luckily, there was only one day when this happened. On that day the driver gave us a good tour around the area before spending the afternoon at the pub for some liquid refreshment with us. The resort was in its infancy at this time with a very small hut doubling up as a take away shop where hot pies etc. could be bought along with hot drinks made from the urn of hot water. Pretty basic to say the least. Having googled Mt Hutt it is now looking like a five star snowfield. I wonder what has been done to counter the ridge to get people there on the very windy days.

Comfortable on the intermediate slopes, I stayed away from the slope for the experts. My mates were good enough to tackle this which had the name of the Shirt Front. On the last day my mates convinced me that I should give it a try, and I thought that as I was here I should give it a go before we left. So I ventured to the T-bar that was the access and took the ride up there. Skiing across the short ridge to get to the start of the run I then realised when looking down the slope why it had the name which it had, a shirt front alright. I carefully took off traversing almost at right angles to the slope to make my way down. The slope got less steep after a while and then I was confident enough to enjoy the rest of the ride, and the moguls on the way down were particularly enjoyable. I went back once more for another run but that was enough for one day as the time to return down the mountain was upon us.

The next day we had a flight from Christchurch across the Southern Alps to Queenstown for the second week of our holiday. Our accommodation at Queenstown was a similar deal to Methven except this time we stayed at a motel. There was a mini bus again to take us from the motel to the slopes of Coronet Peak, not too far away. There was a problem when we got there on the first morning because the level of snow was only good enough for the beginners' run to be in use. It would have been useless to stay on the mountain all day with so little snow there so we headed back to town and spent the day checking out the places to enjoy. Queenstown was a nice place to visit for a few days anyway. A flight back to Sydney ended a real good holiday even though only the first week allowed any skiing.

Sydney, NSW

Arriving back in Sydney I continued working at the North Sydney building site until the end of the year. Then I decided to have a shot at some more country work to refuel my bank balance to do some more travelling. A job in the Sydney Morning Herald interested me, on the new pipeline bringing natural gas to Young in NSW, from Moomba in South Australia.

I had now been working and travelling for almost ten years, since becoming a Ten Pound Pom, and the jobs were still just as plentiful now as they were at the beginning. I went to western Sydney for an interview with the company and was hired to join a four man crew at Cobar in the far west of NSW to start work there in the New Year. Christmas was spent with my mates and when the New Year arrived it was pack up time for pastures new once again.

1976

Cobar, NSW

The day after New Year's Day I went to the office where I had been interviewed for the job and met the two other guys, both fitters, who made up the crew for Cobar. We drove the 650 kilometres to Cobar in a 4x4 ute to meet up with the fourth guy, a trade assistant. Our first night was spent at the town pub, with a trip out of town to the work site next morning. A caravan for accommodation had already been set up for us on site. There was a small shed to be erected which would house a gas-fuelled generator for electricity to power the gas valve operations, and we had ten days for completion of the job. From there we would move to another site along the gas pipeline and another valve etc. to be installed. For our water, we had a tank the correct size to fit in the cargo tray of the 4x4, which had to be filled at the council yard in Cobar. This was quite ironic because about three or four days into the job the rains came down. They were constant and the paddocks became inundated with water about a foot deep. The ground was very flat so the water had nowhere to flow away to, which meant we were waterlogged for day after day.

After two or three days of this we decided on a night out from the site. We had been into Cobar once for a night at the RSL club but on this occasion we had a trip in another direction into a small place called Tilpa on the bank of the Darling River, where there was a small pub. Being honest, most of my time at Tilpa was spent phoning friends in Sydney from the post office phone box. The flooding was extensive and in the twilight the number of kangaroos on the higher ground was uncountable.

The four of us were on full pay, unable to do any work until the flooding subsided, so the supervisor came to tell us the job was suspended, and to go back to Sydney until further notice. The three of us left the next day in the 4x4, driving through sheets of water and large puddles. After a couple of hours I was asked to drive for a while, and had a very bad experience, when the wheels hit a huge puddle at the side of the road. The two wheels on that side aquaplaned and I had no control whatsoever on the steering. The bloke sitting next to me yelled out not to touch the brakes. Thankfully, the stretch of road there was straight and the 4x4 held its course. It was with relief that I felt the wheels in contact with the road again. That was a very scary few seconds and it did not take long for me to be relieved of the driving. Perhaps I should have realised there might be a problem with the water puddles but anyway I did get the experience, and kept that situation in mind. It was quite late when I made my way back to North Sydney for a welcome sleep at the house in Neutral Bay.

It only took me a few days to seek out a replacement job working away, and once again I found a job in the Sydney Morning Herald, working for a mining company based at Tennant Creek. So I collected flight tickets and left a couple of days later for another stint in the Northern Territory.

Tennant Creek, NT

At the airport I was met by a man from the company which had a number of mines in the area. The accommodation at Tennant Creek was pretty old and Spartan and I was not really looking forward to a long stay there. However, the manager of the camp came to tell me I would be going to the Warrego mine next day, on the daily bus servicing the mine from Tennant Creek. I had stayed at Warrego camp before, and knew it was more modern than others I had stayed in previously.

I spent my first morning at the mine doing an induction course and getting safety instructions. The mine was an underground operation and my first sampling of that was to do an emergency egress with one of the shift bosses. The mine had a cage shaft servicing all the levels. The exact number of levels I am unsure of. With the cage shaft sinking down into the ground for a few hundred feet he took me down to about Level 7 where we left the cage and went to the emergency egress ladders. These were simply wooden extension ladders lashed together and connecting each level to the one above. He led the way, at a cracking pace I might add, up through three levels before he stopped. I was absolutely knackered at this point and more than happy that he had decided that I had done enough to show that I was OK with confined spaces and the heights we had to scale on the ladders. I am sure the shift boss was chuckling to himself at having just about worn me out. Little did he know that the only reason I had managed to keep up with him was because I was frightened to death of being left behind in a very uncomfortable environment! As it turned out I did very little work underground, being delegated mainly to jobs in the workshops and around the surface, much like my work at Mount Isa Mines in earlier times. I stayed on here for about four months before I decided to go back to Sydney and work out what my next movement would be. Little did I know it, but my life was about to change, back in Sydney.

Sydney, NSW

The house at Neutral Bay was full, so as I now had a healthy bank balance again I decided to set myself up in a nice flat until I got sorted out. Soon after moving into a studio apartment at Blues Point on the North Shore, not much more than a stroll away, I found a job. I was working on maintenance at, of all places, the

Sydney Morning Herald. This newspaper had been so influential on my working time in Australia I feel like this was fate. I stayed in Sydney just enjoying the night life and things to do, when out of the blue I met my future wife a very short time afterwards.

We met in August, got engaged in September and were married in January 1977. Four terrific kids followed. My travelling was then curbed somewhat but not entirely of course, but then all of that maybe is another story.

A view over looking Shaw, Lancashire taken in 1965. The small town of cotton mills where I attended school and spent most of my time as an adult before emigrating to Australia in February 1966.

Taken in mid 1966 on a scenic flight over the Snowy Mountains of NSW, viewing the dams and lakes which were created by work done for 'The Snowy Mountain Scheme' for Hydro Power and Irrigation

A photo taken at Mount Isa in Queensland at Christmas time 1967. The mine site is seen at the rear of the photo on the skyline.

Thredbo Village, NSW. Photo taken from the Ski lift during a holiday there in 1967.

Outside of the family home during my return in 1968. A defining moment!

At the Exmouth, Western Australia, Gala Week horse racing day September 1969.

Butchery at Djbouti, East Africa. Heading to Athens, Greece from Perth WA 1970

The first camp at Cologne, Germany on the way from England to India en-route to Australia by tour bus, 1970.

Brewery wagon in the city of Munich, Germany during Octoberfest 1970

One of the many outstanding Mosques that grace Isfahan, Iran 1970.

Ready to move onward after an overnight stay at Kandahar, Afghanistan 1970

One hour later on the journey to Kabul, all 28 of us crawled out of this, incredible luck.

The Colosseum Rome, Italy 1970

Erechtheion, a Temple at the Acropolis, Athens, Greece 1970.

Fun and games at the Devils Marbles in the Northern Territory, Australia 1970.

Australian Aboriginals perform at a corroboree in Central Australia. North of Alice Springs in the Northern Territory, 1973.

Mt Hutt ski slopes on the south island of New Zealand, 1975.

A grand old hotel at Wee Waa near Narrabri, NSW 1975.

Bob while working at the Warrego Mine in the Northern Territory, Australia, 1975.